Exeter Medieva
General Editor :

JUDITH

Edited by

B. J. TIMMER

UNIVERSITY OF EXETER

First published in Methuen's Old
English Library, London, 1952.

This revised edition, University of Exeter, 1978.
Second Impression 1982
Third Impression 1988

ISBN   0   85989 058 9

Printed in Great Britain by
Short Run Press Ltd., Exeter

PREFACE

THERE is perhaps no need to offer any explanation for a new edition of *Judith*, for the last separate edition appeared in 1904 and since then not much critical attention has been bestowed upon the poem.

The present edition is based on a careful examination of the manuscript. It differs from its predecessors in that I have accepted some of the suggestions for the arrangement of lines made by J. C. Pope in *The Rhythm of Beowulf*.

I am grateful to the General Editors of this series, Professor F. Norman and Professor A. H. Smith, for their helpful criticism, and to Dr George Kane for reading the Introduction in typescript.

B. J. TIMMER

LONDON
October, 1951

PREFACE TO THIS EDITION

THIS edition incorporates those revisions made by the late B. J. Timmer prior to his death in 1961. In addition the bibliography has been revised and brought up to date.

M. J. S.

EXETER
August, 1977

PREFACE

THERE is little to add to the preparation for a new edition of little for the 11th impression edition appeared in ... and since that not much ...

... Departing ...

... that I have accepted some of his ... for the ...

... ... Pop. I. ...

J. H. CHAMBER

March 195...

PREFACE TO THIS EDITION

HIS edition incorporates the corrections made by ... at ... Turner prior to his death in 19... the addition the bibliography had been revised and brought up to date ...

CONTENTS

ABBREVIATIONS

BTSu . . .	J. Bosworth and T. N. Toller, *An Anglo-Saxon Dictionary* (with Supplement).
Beow . . .	*Beowulf*, ed. F. Klaeber.
D	*Beowulf and Judith*, ed. by E. Van Kirk Dobbie.
ELH . . .	*English Literary History*.
ELN . . .	*English Language Notes*.
ES . . .	*English Studies*.
Foster . .	J. Gregory Foster, *Judith* (1892).
Girvan . .	R. Girvan, *Angelsaksisch Handboek*, Haarlem 1932.
Grein-Köhler	C. W. M. Grein, *Sprachschatz der angelsächsischen Dichter*, ed. J. J. Köhler.
JEGP . . .	*Journal of English and Germanic Philology*.
OHG . . .	Old High German.
Klaeber . .	*Beowulf*, ed. F. Klaeber.
LG . . .	B. J. Timmer, *The Later Genesis* (1948).
Luick . . .	K. D. Luick, *Historische Grammatik der englischen Sprache*, Leipzig 1921, etc.
MLN . . .	*Modern Language Notes*.
MLR . . .	*Modern Language Review*.
Mossé . . .	F. Mossé, *Manuel de l'Anglais du Moyen Age*, Paris 1945.
Nb . . .	Northumbrian.
NED . . .	*A New English Dictionary on Historical Principles*.
NM . . .	*Neuphilologische Mitteilungen*.
OE . . .	Old English.
ON . . .	Old Norse.
OSax . . .	Old Saxon.
PrGerm . .	Primitive Germanic.
Pope . . .	J. C. Pope, *The Rhythm of Beowulf* (1942).
RES . . .	*Review of English Studies*.
SB . . .	K. Brunner, *Altenglische Grammatik nach der angelsächsischen Grammatik von Eduard Sievers*, Halle 1951.
Sisam . . .	K. Sisam, *Studies in the History of Old English Literature* (1953).
WSax . . .	West Saxon.
ZfdA . . .	*Zeitschrift für deutsches Altertum*.

INTRODUCTION

I. The Manuscript

JUDITH is preserved in MS Cotton Vitellius A XV in the British Museum, pp. 202a–209b, according to the latest numbering. It is the last poem in the manuscript and follows immediately upon *Beowulf*. The same hand that wrote *Beowulf* from line 1939b *moste* onwards (the second scribe of *Beowulf*) also wrote our poem, as was first pointed out by Sievers.[1] Yet, as R. W. Chambers pointed out, the two poems probably have not always been together in one book. ". . . the last page of *Beowulf* was apparently once the last page of the volume, to judge from its battered condition, whilst *Judith* is imperfect at the beginning."[2] The date of the manuscript is now generally assumed to be round about the year 1000, but nothing is known with any degree of certainty about its provenance. Förster[3] favours the south of England and, as we shall see later on (p. 10 f), there are perhaps other pointers in the same direction.

In the seventeenth century *Judith* was copied by Franciscus Junius (1589–1677), librarian to the Earl of Arundel and tutor to the Earl's son. This copy of *Judith* is now in the Bodleian Library (MS Junius 105). Madan describes it in the *Catalogue of Western Manuscripts*:

> 5216. In Old English, on paper; written by Francis Junius in the mid-17th cent. in England: 8¼ × 6¼ ins. viii + 20 pages, of which pp. i–viii and 13–20 are blank.
> A fragment of the history of Judith, copied by Francis Junius from Cott. MS. Vitell. A XV, p. 199, beg. "Tweode gifena in þys ginnan grunde" (p. 1), hence printed by Edward Thwaites (Oxford 1699).
> Now MS Junius 105.

The edition by Thwaites, referred to by Madan, appeared

---

[1] ZfdA xv. 457; cf Sisam, MLR xi. 337 (=Sisam, pp. 61 ff.); M. Förster, *Die Beowulf Handschrift* 509.

[2] *Beowulf: An Introduction* (Cambridge 1932) 509.

[3] *Op. cit.* 59.

in 1698 (not 1699) and in the Appendix p. 32 Thwaites states that Junius transcribed the poem "Cujus (i.e. Junii) etiam cura & labore illud fragmentum historiae Judith Bibliotheca Cottoniana descriptum fuit". Junius's transcript is on the whole more correct than Thwaites' edition, but neither shows much care in reproducing the þ and ð of the manuscript accurately. The more important of their deviations have been noted in the textual notes. Thwaites, influenced perhaps by MS Junius 11, put in regular dotting on his own.[1]

Wanley's *Catalogue* 218 ff describes it as follows:

> Fragmentum Poeticum Hist. Judithae Holofernis, Saxonice ante Conquaest. scriptum. Quod descripsit cl. Junius, e cujus Apographo illud typis edidit Edwardus Thwaitesius, in libro suo supra (p. 97) laudato.

Junius's transcript and Thwaites' edition are of particular value, because the manuscript was damaged in the fire at Ashburnham House in 1731. The damage is specially noticeable at the beginning of the pages. The last few lines of the poem are cramped on the end of the manuscript, now almost illegible. No doubt that last page was originally the last of the volume too.

The poem is a fragment: we have only the last part of section IX, further sections X, XI, XII.[2] From the average number of lines in the last three sections the length of the complete poem may be estimated at about 1,344 lines. One arrives at the same result by computing the whole from the length of what is lost in the original source; the first eleven chapters form the first part of the poem, so about three-quarters are lost.[3]

II. LANGUAGE

It has been held for a long time that *Judith* was originally written in an Anglian dialect and that it passed through one

---

[1] See D., pp. xxii f.

[2] Cf Timmer 'Sectional Divisions of Poems in Old English Manuscripts', MLR xlvii, 1952.

[3] See D., pp. lix ff. But see R. E. Woolf, JEGP 50, 1955, pp. 168 ff.

or more hands to be finally written down in the late West Saxon period. The last editor, A. S. Cook,[1] took Northumbria as the original home and printed a Northumbrian transcription. Förster,[2] too, points to an Anglian original. Foster, for reasons mentioned below, assumes that the poem was written down in Mercia.[3] The latest statement to this effect is Professor Kemp Malone's in Baugh, *A Literary History of England* (1949) 68: "We take him to be an Angle of the ninth century, but he may have lived later." A new investigation of the language will lead to different results.

LATE WEST SAXON FEATURES:

hwæne 52, *gehwæne* 186, cf SB 341, note 2.

wiggend 69, etc. The spelling *ig* for *ī* is late WSax, cf SB 24 note; Klaeber, *Beowulf* lxxiv, 5, note 1.

nēhste 73. WSax *ēa* is smoothed to *ē* in late WSax before *h* (*c*, *ȝ*), cf SB 121. Cf *hēhstan* 4, *bēhðe* 174. *ēa* is kept in *bēagum* 36, *beaga* 341; *bēahhrodene* 138; *nēah* 287.

mihte 75. A late WSax form for earlier *meahte*, cf SB 425.

genyðerad 113; late WSax *y* for *i*, cf SB 22, note 2. Similarly, *hyt* 174, *hyre*, *hyne*, *hyra* 127, etc; *syððan* 114; *ys* 86, etc; *þyssa* 187; *þysne* 90, etc; *þyder* 129. Later WSax *ȳ* for *īe* is found in *þȳstrum* 118; *fȳnd* 195; *hȳhsta* 308.

wealgate 141, with *a* from the plural, see SB 240, note 2. Cf *-geates* 162.

swyrd 230, etc. Before *r* + consonant the combination *weo* in late WSax becomes *wu*.

Because of the change of *wyr-* to *wur-* we also find the inverted spelling *wyr-* for *wur- weor-*; cf SB 118, note 1, 113a and note 1. Hence *swyrd*, but the normal WSax *sweord* also occurs (89, 337, etc). Similarly, *þoncwyrðe* 153, as against *geweorðod* 298; *weorðmynde* 342, cf *sweoran* 106; *sweorcend-ferhðe* 269; *sweotole* 177, but *-swutelod* 285.

---

[1] *Judith*, second revised and enlarged edition, Boston 1904, xv. Cf also his edition in the Belles Lettres Series, 1904, viii.

[2] M. Förster, *Die Beowulf Handschrift* 32 and note 1.

[3] J. Gregory Foster, *Judith* (1892) 49.

JUDITH

sylfre 335; *sylfes* 349. Forms with *y*, the only ones which occur, are post-Alfredian; cf SB 124.

o instead of *a* before nasals. There is almost an equal proportion of forms with *o* as against those with *a*.

NON-WSAX FORMS:

pēgon 19. The pret. plural of strong verbs of class V has WSax *ǣ*, Anglian and Kentish *ē*; the *Vespasian Psalter* also has *ē*. Such forms with *ē* (cf also *wēgas*, *Wanderer* 46, for WSax *wǣgas*) cannot be adduced as proofs of Anglian origin, for many of the OE poems were written down in the language of the Worcester scriptorium in the tenth century, and we know that it spread far south and eastwards, cf *gēsne* 112 below.

gēsne 112. Cf OHG *geiseni*. PrGerm *ai* became *ā* and then *ǣ* by *i*-mutation. In Kentish *ē* is found for this sound, but also in the *Vespasian Psalter*, so that again the *ē* may be due to the language of the Worcester scriptorium, cf *pēgon* 19, above.

orfeorme 271. The etymology is obscure. If it is taken with NED as a development from PrGerm *ferma*, it would be regular WSax. If the stem has had an *i*, then *i* broke before *r* + consonant, giving *io*, which in WSax became *eo*.

nēosan 63. Cf Gothic *niuhseins*. *iu* became *īo*, which remained in Nb and Kentish. In Mercian *īo* is rare, *ēo* being the commoner form. In early WSax *īo* is found (cf the cases in the *Later Genesis*, where early WSax *īo* was altered by the corrector into late WSax *ēo*; my ed. p. 21), in late WSax *ēo*.

ēowdon 240. Cf *Beowulf*, ed. Klaeber, lxxiii, § 3, 2. The form *eoweð* occurs *Beowulf* line 1738. The *Vespasian Psalter* also has *ēo* by the side of *ēa* here. The form with *ēo* occurs in WSax.

heaðo- 179; *beaduwe* 175; *beado-* 276. These forms, which show Mercian back-mutation of *a* to *ea*, cannot be taken as evidence of an Anglian original. They should be seen as traditional words, appearing in WSax from the early Anglian poetry. Similarly *waldend*, *alwalda*, *aldor* (line 32),

4

wald 206, to *aldre* 120 (but *ealdre benæman* 76, where the word is not used in a formula).

bælc 267. In strict WSax the word would be **bielc*, with *i*-mutation of *ea*. The word occurs only here and *Genesis* 54, on both occasions with *forbigan*. The poet of *Judith* probably knew this formula.

stercedferhð 227. The first element of this compound occurs with *æ* at *Andreas* 1235, *Elene* 38. In WSax there would have been breaking, with *ea* for Anglian *æ*. Now the *Later Genesis* (cf LG 27), written down in WSax about 900 or shortly afterwards, has two cases of *æ* for *ea*: *hwærf* 240, *folcgestælna* 271. This poem probably never went through Anglian hands. There are also some cases of confusion between *e* and *æ* in the *Later Genesis* (*op. cit* 24). The *e* in *stercedferhð* may also be explained as *e* written for *ea=æ*, due to the language of the Worcester scriptorium; cf *Maldon* (ed. E. V. Gordon 38) 63 *eastede*, 276 *leg*, 279 *wrec;* 113 *-ræste*, 127 *stædefæste*.

Förster (*op. cit*. 32 and note 1) mentions a number of other forms which according to him may be due to an earlier exemplar in a non-WSax dialect. The uncontracted forms (ll.96, 197) do not prove Anglian origin, see Sisam, pp. 123 ff.

It appears then that the language of *Judith* is mainly late WSax, not too far removed from the Alfredian period (see above under *nēhste* 72 and *swyrd* 230). There are no traces of early WSax. The non-WSax forms may be due to the fact that the poem was written down in the tenth-century language of the Worcester scriptorium in the south of England. There is nothing in the text that warrants the assumption of an Anglian origin.

There remains the possibility that the poem was transcribed from an Anglian original into West Saxon. E. V. Gordon (*op.cit*. 40) assumes such a transcription for *Maldon*. But the language of *Maldon* is entirely late WSax and the poem is also written down in the language of the Worcester scriptorium (cf Gordon, *op.cit*. 39). *Maldon* may have been composed by a West Saxon who had heard of—or been

5

present at—the battle. Moreover, an educated Essex man of the late tenth century may have spoken a dialect that was virtually West Saxon. After all, the only easternism that is left in *Maldon* (*gofol* in line 61) may be a case of dittography. If we do not know of any definitely Anglian associations for *Judith*, it is equally possible to assume that *Judith* was composed in late WSax of the tenth century.

III. DATE

Judith is a good example of the difficulty of assigning a date to Old English poetry, for it has been put at various dates from the seventh to the tenth century or even later. Some of the earlier editors ascribed it to Cædmon, others to Cynewulf or his school. Both these theories may now be rejected on account of the phonological evidence, if not for other reasons.

The first to give a definite date to the poem was Cook, who propounded the theory (ed. 1904, xi) that "the poem of Judith was composed in or about the year 856, in gratitude for the deliverance of Wessex from the fury of the heathen Northmen, and dedicated . . . to the adopted daughter of England, the pride, the hope, the darling of the nation", i.e. Judith, the stepmother of King Alfred, whom Alfred's father Æthelwulf had married on the continent in 856. This theory, too, must be rejected, for the state of the language, the metre, and the complete absence of early West Saxon forms point to a much later time. It is moreover difficult to see how the Northern origin—Cook prints a Northumbrian transcription of the poem in his 1904 edition—fits in with the theory that the poem was composed in gratitude for the deliverance of Wessex from the Danes.

In 1892 Foster (*op.cit.* 90 ff) advanced the theory that Judith really represented Queen Æthelflæd of Mercia, Alfred's daughter, and he arrived at the conclusion: "Æthelflæd, then, is Mercia's Judith, for she by no ordinary strategy, we are told, raised her Kingdom and people to their old position. She, like the Hebrew Judith, abandoned the older strategy of raid and battle, not indeed to murder the Danish chief, but to build fortresses and beleaguer her enemies. Æthelflæd, then, is a suitable and worthy heroine to have stirred a contemporary poet to his theme. . . . This suggestion would place our poem between the years 915 and 918 or soon after, during which period she obtained her greatest victories, dying in the last-mentioned year." Though this theory is attractive, and though—as we shall see presently—the date is not impossible, there are objections to it. The Anglo-Saxon Chronicle does not go into raptures over Æthelflæd but simply calls her *Myrcena hlæfdige*, or merely *Æðelflæd*, and only gives information about her deeds. Not till the twelfth century do we find her treated as a heroine. William of Malmesbury (ed. Stubbs I. 136) calls her "fauor civium, pauor hostium" and Henry of Huntingdon (ed. T. Arnold 158) even writes a dithyrambic poem about her. Pre-Conquest England was not given to hero-worship. There is, then, no justification for assuming that Judith stands for Æthelflæd and this theory can certainly not be added in favour of Mercian origin of the poem, for a West Saxon, who had been with Alfred and later remained in the service of his daughter, might have written the poem.

There is, moreover, another objection that may be raised against Foster's theory. *Judith* belongs to the type of poetry to which *Juliana* and *Elene* belong, the religious epic describing the deeds of a fighting saint. In this kind of poetry the religious element was of paramount importance. Judith is saved, like Elene and Juliana, by the firmness of her Christian belief and her trust in God. The person is glorified in this poetry only on account of his or her belief. The religious strength of the heroines of these poems is placed in the foreground. This makes it very unlikely that a religious heroine like Judith would represent a secular queen, like Æthelflæd. But there was in the tenth century another kind of poetry devoted to secular figures. To this belong the poems in the Chronicle, *Brunanburh, Eadmund, Edgar,* the *Death of Ælfred* and *Edward,* as well as *Maldon* (991). These poems were written to commemorate a single worldly event in history. As Campbell (*Brunanburh* 37) remarks: "Such poems must have been a popular form of composition with certain poets of the age." With the exception, possibly of *Brunanburh*, certainly of *Maldon*, their literary value is virtually negligible.

Thus we find in the tenth century two types of poetry: the poems dealing with certain historical events, panegyrics on historical figures, describing their worldly deeds and based on the heroic epic of former times, and on the other hand *Judith*, the religious epic, describing a saint in her religious deeds. There is no evidence that in the tenth century—or in any previous century, for that matter—poems were written about religious figures which symbolized historical figures. *Judith* represents the religious epic of a former period, just as *Maldon* represents the heroic epic of former times. On these grounds we reject Foster's theory that Judith represents Æthelflæd, and with it the Mercian origin of the poem is rejected, which agrees with the phonological evidence. But the possibility that our poem was inspired or suggested by the attacks of the Danes remains. It may have been written, as Brandl (*Literaturgeschichte* in Paul's *Grundriss* 1091) remarks, "to exhort man and woman to the utmost resistance, in the same way as *Maldon*", but also, we would like to add, to strengthen their belief and trust in God.

IV. Metre

The metre of *Judith* shows some irregularities that may have a bearing on the date of the poem. Campbell (*op.cit.* 33) remarks that in tenth-century poetry *g* and *ȝ* cannot be proved to alliterate. In *Judith*, however, *g* and *ȝ* do alliterate:

13. *Judith | gleaw*   22. *goldwine gumena | gytesalum*

123. on account of line 13 we may assume double alliteration in the first half-line: *Judith æt guðe | Gode*

132. *Judith gingran sine | gegnum*

238. *ongeaton | grame*

256. *Judith | galmoda*

Doubtful are lines 2, 9, 112, 149.

There is one case in which the alliteration is not in the first lift of the second half-line: 273 *hogedon þa eorlas* with vowel-alliteration in the first half-line. Lines 200, 212, 231, 243 are doubtful, for the verbs may be taken in unstressed anacrusis.

Double alliteration occurs in lines 78, 83, 85, etc, all in the form *a b a b*, which is proportionally more than in *Beowulf* (over 100 cases, see Klaeber, *Beowulf*, lxx).

Enjambment occurs in lines 1/2, 14/15, 28/29, etc, again more than in *Beowulf* proportionally (some 200 cases, see Klaeber, *op.cit.* p. lxx).

In some cases the finite verb bears the alliteration in the second half-lines, not the noun or verbal noun: 183, 204 (with double alliteration), 207, etc. In line 55 *sn* alliterates with *st*; cf *st/s* in *Maldon* 271.

There is in our poem a frequent use of rhyme; see 2, 23, 29, 60, etc, to which may be added *e/æ* in line 36. I do not think that 202 can be cited as proof of a Mercian origin on the ground that rhyme would be obtained, if the Mercian form for *gerihte* were restored (so Brandl, *op.cit.* 1091). The most striking thing, however, is the large number of expanded lines.[1] They are lines 2–12, 16–21, 30–34, 54–61, 63–68, 88–99 (with the exception of 96), 132, 272–274, 287–290, 338–349.

All these irregularities in the metre point to the late West Saxon period. Campbell's statement (*op.cit.* 33) that in the tenth century *g* and *ȝ* cannot be proved to alliterate has now to be modified to the *second half* of that century; cf Timmer, *Later Genesis* 54. Kemp Malone (in Baugh, *A Literary History of England* 28) remarks: "*Judith* exemplifies the late stage of the run-on style", and refers to his article in RES xix. 201–204. There are, however, some other considerations which will help in dating the poem rather more precisely.

As we have seen, there is a total lack of early West Saxon forms or traces of such forms in *Judith*. In the *Later Genesis*, which was composed about 900 or soon after and copied about the year 1000 in MS Junius 11, we still find early West

[1] Cf Timmer 'Expanded Lines in Old English Poetry', *Neophilologus* xxxv, 226–230.

9

Saxon forms (see LG, *op. cit.* 21 ff). If *Judith* belonged to the same period or to an earlier one, we should expect at least some traces of early West Saxon forms. Now when we consider the proportion of *o* or *a* before nasals—in *Judith* about 29 *o* to 32 *a*—we may say that *Judith* belongs to the first half of the tenth century, when in West Saxon (and Kentish) *a* became more and more frequent before a nasal, until it became almost exclusively used in the period of Ælfric. If the poem is of Mercian origin, there would surely have been a greater proportion of *o*'s before nasals. The metre points to this period, too, as also the frequent use of article + adjective + noun, as in line 3 *æt ðam mæran þeodne*. In the older poetry this use was less frequent. In prose it became quite regular in the course of the tenth century. The first half of the tenth century as the date of our poem fits in very well with this syntactical peculiarity.

This period, however, can be limited down even more. In the passage describing the eagle hovering over the battlefield (lines 205–212), the adjectives *urigfeðera, salowigpada* and *hyrnednebba* are used of the eagle. Of these *urigfeðera* occurs in two well-known earlier poems, *Elene* 29, 111, *Seafarer* 25; *salowigpada* is found applied to the raven in *Fortunes of Men* 37, and in *Brunanburh* 61; *hyrnednebba* only in *Judith* and *Brunanburh* 62. Of these poems only *Elene* and *Brunanburh* give similar descriptions of the eagle, the raven and the wolf on the battlefield. As *Elene* is earlier than *Judith*, and as *Brunanburh* is a very artificial poem, which for its vocabulary draws largely upon older Old English poetry, it seems likely that the words *urigfeðera, salowigpada* and *hyrnednebba* were taken over by the *Brunanburh* poet from older poetry like *Elene*, but in the case of *hyrnednebba* this would point to the fact that *Judith* was composed *before Brunanburh* (937).

Thus we arrive at the conclusion that *Judith* may be dated round about 930, but before 937.

A few words may be added on the relationship between *Judith* and the *Later Genesis*. There are certain indications that the poet of *Judith* knew the *Later Genesis* (i.e. *before* it

10

was inserted in the longer poem, generally called *Genesis* A,
for this insertion was probably not made until MS Junius 11
was written down (cf. L.G., 15)). The word *hreowigmod*
occurs only in *Judith* and the *Later Genesis*. *Hearra*, in
the sense of 'lord', is frequent in the *Later Genesis*, but it is
also found in *Judith* 56 (and in *Maldon* 204). Similarly,
gingra 'servant' is the feminine form of *geongra*, which occurs
in the *Later Genesis*. The compounds *galferhð* (62) and *galmod*
(256) have *gāl-* as a first element, as in *galscipe*, LG 341;
otherwise -*gal* only occurs as the second element of a
compound. To these may be added some words discussed
in the notes, *fylgan* 33; *on lustum* 161; perhaps *hinsið* 117;
geweorðan + acc. 260.

The large number of expanded lines in *Judith* (see p. 9
above) may well point to familiarity with the *Later Genesis*,
for *Judith* is the only tenth-century poem with such a large
proportion of expanded lines.

V. LITERARY APPRECIATION

In spirit *Judith* belongs to the religious epics, especially
those dealing with the life of a female saint, such as *Elene*
and *Juliana*. Its vocabulary shows the same characteristic:
the use of stereotyped epic phrases common to that type of
poetry. The kennings for God are those known from other
religious epics, *frymða Waldend, dugeða Waldend, swegles
weard*, etc: for 'lord' we find *gumena baldor, wigena baldor,
rinca baldor*, etc, all known from heroic poetry. The epic
formula *gefrægen ic* occurs twice. On the whole the remin-
iscences of the Germanic spirit are less prominent in *Judith*
than in earlier religious epics. Apart from the use of the
kennings for 'lord' we may note that Holofernes has a
retinue of warriors who conduct him to his tent (69 ff) and
who are called *eorlas* and *beornas*: Holofernes' feast is dis-
tantly reminiscent of the revelry in a Germanic hall, with
this important difference, that in *Judith* the feast is a dis-
orderly one. The warriors are actually called *bencsittende* and
fletsittende; their armour is that of the Germanic warriors:
byrne, helm, sweord, scild (and its synonyms), etc, with the

cumbol and the *guðfana*; the battle is called *æscplega, ecgplega* or *swyrdgeswing*; the kennings for the warriors are the familiar ones, *byrnwiga, cumbolwiga*, etc; we even find the Germanic method of fighting in a *scildburh*. In these things the poem owes much to the religious epics. The poet may be assumed to have been familiar with the *Cædmonian poems, Andreas*, the Cynewulf poems, the *Later Genesis* and *Beowulf*, as may be seen from the notes to the text. A possible reminiscence of an incident in *Beowulf* is in lines 273 ff, where the poet says that the heathen warriors intended to rouse Holofernes, but *him wiht ne speow*. We may compare Wiglaf's attempt to revive Beowulf with water, but *him wiht ne speow* (*Beowulf* 2854). There is, however, no indication of the *comitatus*-idea: when the warriors find Holofernes dead, they take to their heels. On the whole the distance between Judith and her Hebrew followers, or between Holofernes and his followers, is much greater than between a Germanic lord and his retainers, even though the terminology is retained: the men are called *ðegnas* and Holofernes is *sinces brytta*. One characteristic feature in descriptions of a battle was taken over from older poetry. In his description of the battle (205–212) the traditional wolf, raven and eagle are introduced, who are eager for prey; cf *Genesis* 1442–49; *Exodus* 164; *Elene* 110 ff; *Brunanburh* 61 ff; *Finnsburg* 34; *Beowulf* 3024 ff; also *Maldon* 106 and cf the allusion in *Wanderer* 82.

Yet, in spite of this conventional side of the poem, it has been lavishly praised from the days of Sharon Turner down to the latest edition of Sweet's *Anglo-Saxon Reader*, where the poem is called "one of the noblest in the whole range of Old English poetry". Such high praise is no doubt due to the picture of Judith as a human being and to the vividness of the descriptions. The drinking scene (17–32), Judith's prayer (83–94), the battlefield (205 ff), the battle (199 ff), all these are depicted with gusto and exuberance. The poet is fond of putting in details which give reality to his descriptions, such as the *fleohnet* round Holofernes' bed, the two blows with which Judith kills Holofernes, the rejoicing of the crowd at

the news of Holofernes' death, the fear and excitement of
the Assyrians as they are waiting outside Holofernes' tent
(267–275). These descriptions show the poet's fondness for
realistic detail. In this respect special attention may be
drawn to the poet's attempt to put in some ironical effect.
When the Assyrians are waiting for Holofernes to come out
of his tent and lead them in the battle they are described as
'coughing', no doubt to attract his attention, for they do
not know that he is dead, and in the next lines as gnashing
their teeth and tearing their hair and clothes (271 and 281 ff)
in their annoyance at having no success. There can be little
doubt that this detail was put in by the poet with a view to
the humorous effect, but as always when irony occurs in Old
English poetry, it is of a grim nature (cf Timmer 'Irony in
Old English Poetry', *English Studies* xxiv, 171–175).

There are really only two characters in the poem, Judith
and Holofernes. Judith's maid remains very vague. Both
Holofernes and Judith are clearly drawn characters, Holo-
fernes in his cruelty, sinfulness and drunkenness and Judith
in her courage and her goodness. The poet has given Judith
the features of an Anglo-Saxon woman, with everything the
Anglo-Saxons admired in their women. She is white and
shining (*beorht, ælfscinu*), with curly hair (*wundenlocc*); she is
noble and holy, but courageous (*ides ellenrof*) and above all
wise (*gleaw, snotere, searoðoncol, gleawhydig, gearoponcol*).

But though the poem deserves the high praise that has
been bestowed upon it—even if one does not go quite so far as
Henry Sweet did—it is the poet's character that wins it its high
praise more than his art. His style is stereotyped and conven-
tional, there are none of the bold metaphors of the *Wanderer*,
nor is there the deeply moving tone of the *Dream of the Rood*.
Like *Maldon*, it is imitatory in its art, but, as in *Maldon*, one
feels behind it the strong character of the man who made it.

With regard to the source (see 14 f), the Apocryphal Book
of Judith chapters xii. 10 to xvi. 1,[1] it may be remarked that

---

[1] The poet will have known the apocryphal book in the Latin trans-
lation by St. Jerome of Stridon (second quarter of the fourth
century—420).

the poet has reduced the number of characters, for the eunuch Vagao is not mentioned by name, nor are Nebuchadnezzar, Achior and Ozias. Moreover, the poet has only taken the main incidents, namely the Feast, the Slaying of Holofernes, the return to Bethulia, the fight against the Assyrians and their pursuit, winding up with a short description of the spoil and Judith's thanksgiving to God. Some details are faithfully taken over from the source: *in quarto die* xii. 10 in *by feorðan dogore*, line 12; the handing over of Holofernes' head to the maidservant; *per dies autem triginta* xv. 13 in *anes monðes fyrst*, line 324. There are, however, some points of divergence. In the Vulgate (xii. 10), Judith is brought in to Holofernes during the feast, in the poem she is taken to Holofernes after the conclusion of the banquet. Perhaps the poet wanted to stress the sinfulness of excessive drinking, for the drinking habits of the Danes were notorious. So the poet gave a glowing description of the feast and then went on to say how, after his excessive drinking, Holofernes' thoughts turned to the sinful desire for Judith. A minor point of difference is that, whereas there is no battle in the original after the slaying of Holofernes (xiv. 2), in the poem there is a real fight at this point, when Judith has returned to Bethulia (lines 199 ff). In the original the Assyrians are so overcome by fear that they take to their heels at once (xiv. 7–xv. 8). Our poet, however, could not miss the opportunity of giving a wonderfully spirited description of a battle. But apart from these two cases the poet followed the original story, concentrating on the main incidents, but altering the order of events.[1]

VI. RELEVANT PASSAGES FROM THE VULGATE JUDITH

ix. 14. Da mihi in animo constantiam, ut contemnam illum; et virtutem, ut evertam illum.

ix. 17. Deus caelorum, Creator aquarum, et Dominus totius creaturae, exaudi me miseram deprecantem, et de tua misericordia praesumentem (perhaps the passage preceding the text).

x. 16. Duxeruntque illam ad tabernaculum Holofernis, annuntiantes eam (lines 37–55).

[1] See also D., pp. lix f.

RELEVANT PASSAGES FROM THE VULGATE

xii. 10. Et factum est, in quarto die Holofernes fecit coenam servis suis, et dixit ad Vagao eunuchum suum: Vade, et suade Hebraeam illam ut sponte consentiat habitare mecum (lines 7-14).

xii. 16. Cor autem Holofernis concussum est; erat enim ardens in concupiscentia ejus (lines 57ᵇ-60).

xii. 20. Et jucundus factus est Holofernes ad eam, bibitque vinum multum nimis, quantum numquam biberat in vita sua (lines 15-37ᵃ).

xiii. 1-xix. 1. Ut autem sero factum est, festinaverunt servi illius ad hospitia sua, et conclusit Vagao ostia cubiculi, et abiit; erant autem omnes fatigati a vino. Eratque Judith sola in cubiculo; porro Holofernes jacebat in lecto, nimia ebrietate sopitus. . . . Stetitque Judith ante lectum orans cum lacrymis, et labiorum motu in silentio, dicens: confirma me, Domine Deus Israel, et respice in hac hora ad opera manuum mearum . . . ; et hoc, quod credens per te posse fieri cogitavi, perficiam. . . . Pugionem ejus, qui in ea ligatus pendebat, exsolvit. Cumque evaginasset illum, apprehendit comam capitis ejus, et ait: Confirma me, Domine Deus, in hac hora. Et percussit bis in cervicem ejus, et abscidit caput ejus, et abstulit conopeum ejus a columnis, et evolvit corpus ejus truncum (lines 61-121). Et post pusillum exivit, et tradidit caput Holofernis ancillae suae, et jussit ut mitteret illud in peram suam. Et exierunt duae, . . . et transierunt castra, et, gyrantes vallem, venerunt ad portam civitatis. Et dixit Judith a longe custodibus murorum: Aperite portas, quoniam nobiscum est Deus, qui fecit virtutem in Israel. Et factum est, cum audissent viri vocem ejus, vocaverunt presbyteros civitatis. Et concurrerunt ad eam omnes, a minimo usque ad maximum. . . . Dixit Judith: Laudate Dominum Deum nostrum, qui non deseruit sperantes in se; . . . et interfecit in manu mea hostem populi sui hac nocte. Et proferens de pera caput Holofernis, ostendit illis, dicens: Ecce caput Holofernis principis militiae Assyriorum, . . . ubi per manum feminae percussit illum Dominus Deus noster (lines 122-186ᵃ).

xiv. 1, 2. Dixit autem Judith ad omnem populum: Audite me, fratres. . . . Et erit, cum exierit sol, accipiat unusquisque arma sua, et exite cum impetu, non ut descendatis deorsum, sed quasi impetum facientes.

xiv. 4, 5. Cumque duces eorum cucurrerint ad tabernaculum Holofernis, et invenerint eum truncum in suo sanguine volutatum, decidet super eos timor. Cumque cognoveritis fugere eos, ite post illos securi, quoniam Dominus conteret eos sub pedibus vestris (lines 186ᵇ-198).

xiv. 7-xv. 8. Mox autem, ut ortus est dies, . . . accepitque unusquisque vir arma sua, et egressi sunt cum grandi strepitu et ululatu (lines 199-235). Quod videntes exploratores, ad tabernaculum Holofernis cucurrerunt. Porro hi, qui in tabernaculo erant, venientes, et ante ingressum cubiculi perstrepentes, excitandi gratia, inquietudinem arte moliebantur, ut non ab excitantibus, sed a sonantibus,

15

JUDITH

Holofernes evigilaret. Nullus enim audebat cubiculum virtutis Assyriorum pulsando aut intrando aperire. Sed cum venissent ejus duces ac tribuni, et universi majores exercitus regis Assyriorum, dixerunt cubiculariis: Intrate, et excitate illum, quoniam egressi mures de cavernis suis ausi sunt provocare nos ad praelium. Tunc ingressus Vagao cubiculum ejus, stetit ante cortinam, et plausum fecit manibus suis; suspicabatur enim illum cum Judith dormire. Sed cum nullum motum jacentis sensu aurium caperet, accessit proximans ad cortinam, et, elevans eam, vidensque cadaver absque capite Holofernis in suo sanguine tabefactum jacere super terram, exclamavit voce magna cum fletu, et scidit vestimenta sua. Et ingressus tabernaculum Judith, non invenit eam, et exiliit foras ad populum, et dixit: Una mulier Hebraea fecit confusionem in domo regis Nabuchodonosor; ecce enim Holofernes jacet in terra, et caput ejus non est in illo. Quod cum audissent principes virtutis Assyriorum, sciderunt omnes vestimenta sua, et intolerabilis timor et tremor cecidit super eos, et turbati sunt animi eorum valde. Et factus est clamor incomparabilis in medio castrorum eorum. Cumque omnis exercitus decollatum Holofernem audisset, fugit mens et consilium ab eis, et, solo tremore et metu agitati, fugae praesidium sumunt; ita ut nullus loqueretur cum proximo suo, sed, inclinato capite, relictis omnibus, evadere festinabant Hebraeos, quos armatos super se venire audiebant, fugientes per vias camporum et semitas collium (lines 236–297[a]). Videntes itaque filii Israel fugientes, secuti sunt illos. Descenderuntque clangentes tubis, et ululantes post ipsos. Et quoniam Assyrii non adunati, in fugam ibant praecipites; filii autem Israel uno agmine persequentes, debilitabant omnes quos invenire potuissent. Misit itaque Ozias nuntios per omnes civitates et regiones Israel. Omnis itaque regio omnisque urbs electam juventutem armatam misit post eos, et persecuti sunt eos in ore gladii quousque pervenirent ad extremitatem finium suorum. Reliqui autem, qui erant in Bethulia, ingressi sunt castra Assyriorum, et praedam quam fugientes Assyrii reliquerant abstulerunt; et onustati sunt valde. Hi vero qui victores reversi sunt ad Bethuliam omnia quae erant illorum attulerunt secum, ita ut non esset numerus in pecoribus, et jumentis, et universis mobilibus eorum, ut a minimo usque ad maximum omnes divites fierent de praedationibus eorum (lines 297[b]–323[a]).

xv. 13, 14. Per dies autem triginta, vix collecta sunt spolia Assyriorum a populo Israel. Porro autem universa quae Holofernis peculiaria fuisse probata sunt dederunt Judith, in auro, et argento, et vestibus, et gemmis, et omni suppellectili; et tradita sunt omnia illi a populo.

xvi. 1. Tunc cantavit canticum hoc Domino Judith, dicens: . . . (lines 323[b]–349).

JUDITH

gifena in ðys ginnan gr(un)d(e).   Heo ðær ða gearwe
    fu(n)de
mundbyr(d) æt ðam mæran þeodne,   þa heo ahte
    mæste þearfe
hyldo þæs hehstan Deman,   þæt he hie wið þæs hehstan
    brogan
5 gefriðode,frymða Waldend. Hyre ðæs Fæder on roderum
  torhtmod tiðe gefremede,   þe heo ahte trumne geleafan
  á to ðam Ælmihtigan.   Gefrægen ic ða Holofernus

TEXTUAL VARIANTS: letters that are not legible in the manuscript
but can be supplied from Junius's transcript and Thwaites' edition,
are between ( ). Emendations and additions are between ⟨ ⟩.
Letters in italics represent the expansion of abbreviations.

(2) *ðær*; see note. D. *ðar*.

(7) *ðam*; Junius *ðæm*., Thwaites *þæm*.

---

(1) *Tweode*. The *w* of *tweode* is still legible. This word is the first on
folio 202ᵃ. Cook suggests that *ne* or *no* should be supplied, but that is
not quite certain, as we do not know what came before *tweode*. Cook
argues that in spite of the numbers X, XI and XII, denoting fits,
which appear at 15, 122 and 236, the poem seems virtually complete
as it now is, because the opening lines are echoed at the end of the
fragment, where we find *tweode* in 345ᵇ, and 6ᵇ–7ᵃ = 344ᵇ and 345ᵃ.
This can only be accidental and the division in fits really indicates
that 8 fits and most of fit IX are lost.

(2) With *gifena* taken into this line, it forms a hypermetrical verse.
See Pope, *The Rhythm of Beowulf* 100. Cf 345, where *tweode* also occurs
at the end of a line. *ginnan grunde*: cf *Beow* 1551; *Widsith* 51; and
Judgment Day I 12. *ðær*: The manuscript reads *ðær*, also Junius and
Thwaites, but the loop of the ligature is faded, though still visible. In
the early nineteenth century Thorpe could still read the *æ*, but Sweet
(1874) read *ðar* (14th ed. *ðær*).

(4) *hyldo*: gen.sing., as in the *Later Genesis* 663, *Beowulf* 2998. The
word belongs to the -*īn*- stems, which have a gen.sing. in -*e*, but later
u, o; cf SB 280.

(7) *Holofernus*: this name always alliterates with a vowel. The
name seems to require a long *ō*, as may be concluded from 46ᵃ on
metrical grounds. In l. 250 the alliteration is probably on the vowel.

JUDITH

wínhatan wyrcean georne 7 eallum wundrum þrymlic
girwan up swæsendo: to ðam het se gumena bal(d)or
10 ealle ða yldestan ðegnas. Hie ðæt ofstum miclum
ræfndon rondwiggende, comon to ðam rican þeodne
feran, folces ræswan. Þæt wæs þy feorðan dogore,
þæs ðe Iudith hyne gleaw on geðonce
ides ælfscinu ærest gesohte.
15 Hie ða to ðam symle sittan eodon, X.
wlance to wíngedrince, ealle | (h)is weagesiðas [202b
bealde byrnwiggen(de). Þær wæron bollan steape
boren æfter (b)encum gelome, swylce eac bunan 7 orcas
fulle fletsittendum. Hie þæt fæge þegon,
20 rofe rondwiggende, þeah ðæs se rica ne wende
egesful eorla dryht(en). Ða wearð Holofernus
goldwine gumena on gytesalum.
Hloh 7 hlydde, hlynede 7 dynede,
þæt mihten fira bearn feorran gehyran,
25 hu se stiðmoda styrmde 7 gylede,
modig 7 medugal manode geneahhe
bencsittende, þæt hi gebærdon wel.
Swa se inwidda ofer ealne dæg

---

(12) *dogore*: for metrical reasons Cook reads *dogor*, but the second *o*
was elided in reading, as in *Beow* 1797, 2573; cf *dogora* 88 and *dogera*
823 by the side of *dogra* 1090. Cf Girvan 297: *ræswan* is dat. sing.

(14) *ælfscinu*. The adj. occurs only here and *Genesis* 1827, 2731,
mæg ælfscieno. Grimm (*Mythology* 444): 'Probably then *albs* meant
first of all a light-coloured, white, good spirit.' Cf ON *ljósálfar*. In ON
the sun is called *álfroðull* 'elfin beam of light'. In *Beow* 112, the elves
are mentioned among *evil* spirits.

(18) *æfter* 'along'.

(23) *hlynede 7 dynede*: see above 8; the same rhyme occurs in the
Rhyming Poem 28.

(27) *gebærdon*: cf L. L. Schücking, 'Heldenstolz und Würde im
Angelsächsischen' 21, whose interpretation had already been sug-
gested in 1880 by Körner.

(28) *se inwidda*. In connection with the frequent occurrence of
article and weak adjective (25, 48, etc) it is perhaps best to take this
word as an adjective. It occurs only here and *Brunanburh* 46. BT
compare Gothic *inwids* 'unjust, perverse'. At *Christ and Satan* 727
the manuscript reads *inwitum*, which Krapp and Clubb read as *in
witum*, but it is possible that here too the adjective should be read.

18

JUDITH

dryhtguman sine drencte mid wine,
30 swiðmod sinces brytta, oð þæt hie on swiman lagon,
oferdrencte his duguðe ealle, swylce hie wæron deaðe
geslegene,
agotene goda gehwylces. Swa het se gumena ⟨e⟩aldor
fylgan fletsittendum, oð þæt fira bearnum
nea | (l)æhte niht seo þystre. Het ða niða geblon-
den [203ᵃ
35 þa eadigan mægð ofstum fetigan
to his bedreste, beagum gehlæste,
hringum gehrodene. Hie hraðe fremedon
anbyhtscealcas, swa him heora ealdor bebead,
byrnwigena brego. Bearhtme stopon
40 to ðam gysterne, þær hie Iudithðe
fundon ferhðgleawe, 7 ða fromlice
lindwiggende lædan ongunnon
þa torhtan mægð to træfe þam hean,
þær se rica hyne reste on symbel,

(40) *iudithðe*: Junius *Iuditðe*, Thwaites *Iuditþe*.

---

(32) *aldor.* A *b* is erased (but still clearly visible) before *aldor; baldor*
occurs at 9, 49, 338; *aldor* only occurs in the form with breaking,
ealdor. We may assume that at 32 the *b* was erased in order to make
place for an *e*, which was never inserted. *agotene*, etc: Cook gives
āgēotan 'drain, deprive of'. Grein-Köhler translate the past participle
'entleert, verlustig' (?). So also BT. It is possible to start from a
figurative use of *ageotan* 'to pour out', so that the past participle, used
with the gen., means 'empty of'.

(33) *fylgan*: Cook reads *fyllan* 'fill with wine, pour out', but that is
too modern and does not agree with the dative *fletsittendum*. The
manuscript reading may be kept and the sense may be the same as at
Later Genesis 249, 'to serve'; cf above p. 11.

(39) *bearhtme*: inst. of *bearhtm* 'tumult, noise'. They will have
fetched Judith with much tumult, so this sense is preferred to that
of 'instantly', as assumed in Sweet's *Reader*, which would be a repeti-
tion of *hraðe* in 37.

(40) *gystern*: a compound, formed like *gystsele* in *Beow* 994, *gæsthof*
in *Christ and Satan* 820.

(43) *træf*: in the sense 'tent' the word occurs only in *Jud* and
perhaps in *Andreas* 842, where Krapp translates 'tent, building'.
Otherwise it occurs in compounds, e.g. *heargtræf* in *Beow* 175; *helltræf*
in *Andreas* 1691; *weargtræf* in *Elene* 927, in the sense 'temple, house'.

19

45 nihtes inne,   Nergende laðˇ
   Holofernus.   Þær wæs eallgylden
   fleohnet fæger   7 ymbe þæs folctogan
   bed ahongen,   þæt se bealofulla
   mihte wlitan þurh,   wigena baldor,
50 on æghwylcne   þe ðær inne com
   hæleða bearna   7 on hyne nænig
   monna cynnes,   nymðe se modiga hwæne
   niðe rofra   him þe near het(e)
   rinca to rune gegangan.   Hie ða on reste gebrohton |
55 (sn)ude ða snoteran idese.   Eodon ða ste(rced)-
                                   ferhðe   [203ᵇ
   hæleð heora hearran cyðan,   þæt wæs seo halige meowle
   gebroht on hi(s) burgetelde.   Þa wearð se brema on
                                      mode
   bliðe, burga ealdor, þohte ða beorhtan idese
   mid widle 7 mid womme besmitan.   Ne wolde þæt
                                        wuldres Dema
60 geðafian, þrymmes Hyrde,   ac he him þæs ðinges
                                gestyrde
   Dryhten, dugeða Waldend.   Gewat ða se deofulcunda,
   galferhð gumena ðreate,
   bealofull his beddes neosan,   þær he sceolde his blæd
                                     forleosan

(54)   MS *gebrohten* with *o* above *e* and dot under *e*. Junius, Thwaites *gebrohten*.
(59)   Thwaites *somme*.

---

(47)   Cook and Sweet omit 7 before *ymbe*, but it is possible to take *ahongen* predicatively, like *eallgylden, fæger*; cf *Beow* 49 ff. *fleohnet* occurs only in Glosses, where it is translated by *conopeum vel micgnet* (Wright-Wülcker 48, 57).
(53)   *þe near*: *þe* is pleonastic, like *þon* in *þon maran* 92.
(60)   *gestyrde*: *gestyran* 'to restrain a person from', also occurs in the *Cura Pastoralis* 44, 23; 116, 14: *Orosius* 296, 11. Other examples are given by BTSu, s.v. *gestiran* IIc.
(62)   Other editors supply *gangan* and so make one normal line in the midst of a hypermetrical group. It seems better to leave the text as it is in the manuscript, thus giving one hypermetrical half-line. Perhaps the second half is missing, or else it was never there.

JUDITH

ædre binnan anre nihte. Hæfde ða his ende gebidenne
65 on eorðan unswæslicne, swylcne he ær æfter worhte,
þearlmod ðeoden gumena, þenden he on ðysse worulde
wunode under wolcna hrofe. Gefeol ða wine swa
    druncen
se rica on his reste middan, swa he nyste ræda nanne
on gewitlocan. Wiggend stopon |
70 ut of ðam inne ofstum miclum,   [204ª
wera(s) winsade, þe ðone wærlogan,
laðne leodhatan, læddon to bedde
nehstan siðe. Þa wæs Nergendes
þeowen þrymful, þearle gemyndig,
75 hu heo þone atolan eaðost mihte
ealdre benæman, ær se unsyfra
womfull onwoce. Genam ða wundenlocc,
scyppendes mægð, scearpne mece
scurum heardne 7 of sceaðe abræd
80 swiðran folme. Ongan ða swegles Weard
be naman nemnan, Nergend ealra
woruldbuendra 7 þæt word ácwæð:
"Ic ðe, frymða God 7 frofre Gæst,
Bearn Alwaldan, biddan wylle

(84) Thwaites *wille*.

---

(64) *gebidenne*: the prefix *ge-* makes the sense perfective, 'attained'.

(65) *æfter worhte*: *æfter* is not a preposition with *swylcne*, as BTSu suggests, but *wyrcan æfter* has the meaning 'to strive after, to head for'; so 'such as he had been heading for'.

(73) *nehstan siðe*: 'for the last time', cf *Beow* 1203, 2511, etc.

(77) *wundenlocc*: this word occurs only in *Jud* and in *Riddle* 26, line 11. Tucker (*Riddles* 125 ff) points out that 'curled or braided locks were regarded by the Anglo-Saxon as an accessory of beauty'.

(78) *mece*: OSax *māki*, cf WSax *mæcefisc* (Luick § 189, 1, note). In poetical texts the word always has *ē*, see *Dream of the Rood* (ed. Dickins and Ross), line 48 note.

(79) *scurum heardne*: cf *scurheard* in *Beow* 1033, which Klaeber renders 'hard in the storm of battle', the meaning here; cf *Lay of Hildebrand* 64 *scarpen scûrim*.

85 miltse þinre me þearfendre,
    Ðrynesse Ðrym. Þearle ys me nu ða
    heorte onhæted 7 hige geomor,
    swyðe mid sorgum gedrefed. Forgif me, swegles Ealdor,
    sigor 7 soðne geleafan, þæt ic mid þys sweorde mote
90 geheawan þysne morðres bryttan. Geunne me minra
        ge | synta, [204^b]
    þearlmod Þeoden gumena: naht(e) ic þinre næfre
    miltse þon maran þearf(e). Gewrec nu, mihtig Dryhten,
    torhtmod tires Brytta, þæt me ys þus torne on mode,
    hate on hreðre minum." Hi ða se hehsta Dema
95 ædre mid elne onbryrde, swa He deð anra gehwylcne
    herbuendra, þe Hyne him to helpe seceð,
    mid ræde 7 mid rihte geleafan. Þa wearð hyre rume on
        mode,
    haligre hyht geniwod. Genam ða þone hæðenan man-
        nan
    fæste be feaxe sinum, teah hyne folmum wið hyre
        weard
100 bysmerlice, 7 þone bealofullan
    listum alede, laðne mannan,
    swa heo ðæs unlædan eaðost mihte

(85) MS þearf | fendre.
(87) MS *heorte ys*.
(90) *me* added above the line, with a tag underneath by the same
    hand.
(98) Thwaites *ganam*.

---

(85) *þearfendre*: the manuscript has *þearf* as the last word of one
line and *fendre* as the first word of the next.

(95) *anra gehwylcne*: cf Addenda to Notes in Dickins and Ross,
Dream of the Rood, and the note to line 86 of that poem in Sweet's
Reader (12th ed.).

(96a) Pope adds *heanra* before *herbuendra*, to make the line hyper-
metric (220 note), but l. 96b is not hyper-metric. Line 96 (and perhaps
95b) may well be an addition by a scribe; cf *Daniel* 288, which is not
in *Azarias* after l. 9.

(97b) Cf *Later Genesis* 518 *þe weorð on þinum breostum rum*.

(99) *wið hyre weard*: cf *to us-weard* Ps. 40, 7. BT s.v. *weard* gives
prose examples of *weard* in this use. See NED s.v. *ward*.

wel gewealdan.   Sloh ða wundenlocc
þone feondsceaðan   fagum mece
105 heteþoncolne,   þæt heo healfne forcearf
þone sweoran him,   þæt he on swiman læg
druncen 7 dolhwund.   Næs ða dead þa gyt,
ealles orsawle: sloh ða eornoste
ides ellenróf | (o) þre siðe   [205ᵃ
110 þone hæðenan hund,   þæt him þæt heafod wand
forð on ða flore.   Læg se fula leap
gesne beæftan,   gæst ellor hwearf
under neowelne næs   7 ðær genyðerad wæs
susle gesæled   syððan æfre,
115 wyrmum bewunden,   witum gebunden,
hearde gehæfted   in hellebryne
æfter hinsiðe.   Ne ðearf he hopian nó

(108) *eornoste*: Thwaites *eornost*.

---

(104) *fagum mece*: cf lines 194, 301. Cook translates 'gleaming,
bloodstained (?)'. The latter meaning is not very likely here, as the
blow has not yet been delivered. Sweet suggests 'hostile (?)', but the
sword is not hostile, and in connection with the examples in *Beowulf*
(*fáh* used of a sword), it seems more plausible to assume the meaning
'shining', cf *Beow* 1459, 1615, 2701.

In *Beowulf, fáh* meaning 'bloodstained' is always accompanied by
blóde, swáte, dréore, cf 447, 934, etc.

(110) *þone hæðenan hund*: This contemptuous use of 'dog' goes
back to the Bible, see BTSu s.v. *hund*, and is connected with the con-
ception of the dog as an unclean animal. Cf *Boethius* (ed. W. G. Sedge-
field) 114, 27; *St. Marharete* (ed. F. M. Mack, EETS 1934) 14, 29 *Me,
þu heaðene hund, þe hehe healent is min help.*

(111) *leap*: the word usually means 'basket'; in the sense 'trunk'
it occurs only here.

(113) *under neowelne næs*, cf *Beow* 1411. The adjective *neowol* is
often used in descriptions of hell, as here; cf *Christ and Satan* 31, 90,
etc; *Juliana* 684; *Guthlac* 563; in many cases it is used with *næs*. Cook
compares *Elene* 832, *neolum næsse*.

(114) *susle gesæied*; cf *Andreas* 1379 *susle gebunden*. It is connected
with hell in *Guthlac* 667 *in þæt swearte susl.*

(117) *æfter hinsiðe*: cf *Later Genesis* 717, 720. The word *hinsið* also
occurs in *Guthlac* 1357, etc.   It is not impossible that the word was
taken from the *Later Genesis. hopian*: Foster (88) refers to an article
by Dietrich in ZfdA ix. 216 and points out that *hopian* in poetry only

23

þystrum forðylmed, þæt he ðonan mote
of ðam wyrmsele, ac ðær wunian sceal
120 awa to aldre butan ende forð
in ðam heolstran hám hyhtwynna leas.
Hæfde ða gefohten foremærne blæd   XI.
Iudith æt guðe, swa hyre God uðe,
swegles Ealdor, þe hyre sigores onleah.
125 Þa seo snotere mægð snude gebrohte
þæs herewæðan heafod swa blodig
on ðam fætelse, þe hyre foregenga,
bláchleor ides, hyra begea nest,
ðeawum geðungen, þyder on lædde
130 7 hit | ða (s)wa heolfrig hyre on hond ageaf,   [205^b]
(hige)þoncolre ham to berenne
Iudith gingran sinre. Eodon ða gegnum þanonne
þa idesa bá, ellenþriste,
oð þæt hie becomon collenferhðe,
135 eadhreðige mægð, ut of ðam herige,
þæt hie sweotollice geseon mihten
þære wlitegan byrig weallas blican,

(134) *hie* written twice in the MS.

---

occurs here and in the *Metra* of Boethius 7, 44. The word came into
use late in the ninth century and is the common word for 'hope' in
the tenth century, in earlier poetry the idea being expressed by
wēnan or *hycgan*.

(118) *forðylmed*: Cook translates 'encompass, enwrap', so also
Grein-Köhler. It occurs in the same sense in *Phoenix* 284, *Elene* 767.
BTSu render it 'choke' or 'darkened'. The sense 'enwrap' seems
preferable here.

(122) *gefohten*: With perfective meaning, 'attained by fighting';
similarly *Maldon* 129. In *Beow* 1084 *gefeohtan* means simply 'to
fight'; cf *Jud* 219 *gegan* 'gone', but 331 *geeodon* 'they won'.

(124) *onleah*: preterite of *onlēon* according to class II of the strong
verbs. The verb belongs to the *verba contracta*, which early in WSax
passed over into class II, whereas in Anglian they belonged to class I
(pret. *onlāh*), cf SB 383, 2.

(132) *gingran*: *geongra* in the *Later Genesis* is frequently used for
'servant'. Here we have the feminine *gingre*.

(136) Cook compares *Beow* 221 ff, where the retainers see from afar
the shining cliffs.

JUDITH

Bethuliam.   Hie ða beahhrodene
feðelaste   forð onettan,
140 oð hie glædmode   gegán hæfdon
to ðam wealgate.   Wiggend sæton,
weras wæccende   wearde heoldon
in ðam fæstenne,   swa ðam folce ǽr
geomormodum   Iudithe bebéad,
145 searoðoncol mægð,   þa heo on sið gewat,
ides ellenróf.   Wæs ða eft cumen
leof to leodum   7 ða lungre het
gleawhydig wíf   gumena sumne
of ðære ginnan byrig   hyre togeanes gán
150 7 hi ofostlice   in forleton
þurh ðæs wealles geat   7 þæt word acwæð
to ðam sigefolce: "Ic eow secgan mæg
þoncwyrðe þing,   þæt ge ne þyrfen leng |
(mu)rnan on mode: eow ys Metod bliðe   [206ª
155 cyninga Wuldor.   þæt gecyðed wearð
geond woruld wide,   þæt eow ys wuldorblæd
torhtlic toweard   7 tir gifeðe
þara læðða   þe ge lange drugon."
þa wurdon bliðe   burhsittende,
160 syððan hi gehyrdon   hu seo halige spræc

---

(142) MS *heoildon*. Junius, Thwaites *heo ildon*.
(150) MS *forlęton*, with second *o* altered from *e*; Thwaites *forlæten*.

---

(139) *feðelaste*: in his Glossary Cook explains this form as *acc.plural*, but it is the instrumental or dative *singular*, cf *Beow* 1632 *fērdon forð þonon fēþelāstum*. The acc.plural would be -*lastas*.

(144) The MS reading *iudithe* is either a mistake or a sign of late WSax weakening of unstressed syllables, for it is the subject here.

(149) Cook and Sweet transpose the half-lines for metrical reasons, but this is not necessary. In Judith *g* and *ġ* still alliterate (see above p. 8).

(150) *forlęton*: *o* for *a* in the infinitive ending is also found at line 247 *tobredon*.

(158) *þara læðða*: 'for the sorrows', adverbial genitive. It is not necessary to supply a noun, as earlier editors did.

25

ofer heanne weall.   Here wæs on lustu*m*,
wið þæs fæstengeates   folc onette,
weras wif somod,   wornu*m* 7 heapu*m*,
ðreatu*m* 7 ðry*m*mu*m*   þrungon 7 urnon
165 ongean ða þeo⟨d⟩nes mægð   þusendmælu*m*
ealde ge geonge: æghwylcu*m* wearð
men on ðære medobyrig   mod areted,
syððan hie ongeaton   þ*æt* wæs Iudith cumen
eft to eðle,   7 ða ofostlice
170 hie mid eaðmedu*m*   in forleton.
Þa seo gleawe het   golde gefrætewod
hyre ðinenne   þancolmode
þæs herewæðan   heafod onwriðan
7 hyt to behðe   blodig ætywan
175 þam burhleodu*m*,   hu hyre æt beaduwe gespeow.
Spræc ða seo æðele | (to eal)lu⟨m⟩ þa⟨m⟩folce: [206b
"Her ge magon sweotol(e),   (si)gerofe hæleð,
leoda ræswan,   on ðæs (l)aðestan
hæðenes heaðorinces   heafod staria⟨n⟩,
180 Holofernus   unlyfigendes,
þe us monna mæst   morðra gefremede,
sarra sorga   7 þ*æt* swyðor gyt
ycan wolde;   ac him ne uðe God
lengran lifes,   þ*æt* he mid læððu*m* us

(163) Thwaites *weras 7 wif.*
(165) MS *þeoðnes*, Thwaites *ðeodnes.*
(176) MS *(eal)lu þa.*
(179) MS *stariað*; Junius, Thwaites *starian.*
(182) Junius, Thwaites *and syðor* (Thwaites *þ*) *gýt.*

(161) *on lustum*: the usual formula is in the singular, as in *Andreas* 1023, *Elene* 138. The plural occurs in this phrase only here and in the *Later Genesis* 473.

(165) *þeodnes*: MS *þeoðnes*, with confusion of *d* and *ð*; cf *Beow* 1375 *drysmaþ.* 1107 *ad*, etc. In *Beow* this may be due to an eighth-century confusion of *d* and *ð*, but it occurred later too.

(179) *starian*: the MS reading *stariað* is impossible here; see note to 194.

(181) *monna mæst morðra*: literally 'most of the murders of men', object of *gefremede*. Cf *Widsith* 2 *monna mæst mægða* (as emended), *Beow* 2645 *manna mæst mærþa.*

185 eglan moste: ic him ealdor oðþrong
    þurh Godes fultum. Nu ic gumena gehwæne
    þyssa burgleoda biddan wylle,
    randwiggendra, þæt ge recene eow
    fysan to gefeohte, syððan frymða God,
190 árfæst Cyning, eastan sende
    leohtne leoman. Berað linde forð,
    bord for breostum 7 byrnhomas,
    scire helmas in sceaðena gemong,
    fylla⟨ð⟩ folctogan fagum sweordum,
195 fæge frumgaras. Fynd syndon eowere
    gedemed to deaðe 7 ge dóm agon,
    tír æt tohtan, swa eow getacnod hafað
    mihtig Dryhten þurh mine | (h)and."   [207ᵃ
    Þa wearð snelra werod snude gegearewod,
200 cenra to campe. Stopon cynerofe
    secgas 7 gesiðas, bæron ⟨sige⟩þufas,
    foron to gefeohte forð on gerihte,
    hæleð under helmum of ðære haligan byrig
    on ðæt dægred sylf. Dynedan scildas,
205 hlude hlummon. Þæs se hlanca gefeah
    wulf in walde 7 se wanna hrefn,
    wælgifre fugel; w⟨i⟩stan begen

(187) Thwaites *burhleoda*.
(194) MS *fyllan*. So D.
(201) MS *þufas*. Ettmüller, Sweet [sige]-.
(205) Thwaites *hluin mon*.
(207) MS *westan*.

---

(189) *fysan*: late WSax subj.plural, cf SB 361, note 1, with *a* for *e*.

(194) *fyllað*: MS *fyllan*; Cook explains this as standing for the gerund *tō fyllanne*, which is unusual. Probably the scribe's eye caught the ending -*an* of *folctogan*, just as, conversely, at 179, his eye was caught by the *d* of *heafod*, which caused him to write *stariað*.

(201) ⟨*sige*⟩ *þufas*: *sige*- supplied by Ettmüller and Sweet, because an alliterating word is required in the half-line. As to *þufas*, cf Latin *tufa* in Bede, *Historia Ecclesiastica* II. xvi: *quod Romani tufam, Angli uero apellant tuuf* (*segen* in the OE version). O. S. Anderson, *Old English Material in the Leningrad Manuscript of Bede's Ecclesiastical History* (1941) 79, discusses the word and says that the Latin word is a loan word from Germanic.

þæt him ða þeodguman þohton tilian
fylle on fægum. Ac him fleah on last
210 earn ætes georn, urigfeðera,
salowigpada; sang hildeleoð
hyrnednebba. Stopon heaðorincas,
beornas to beadowe, bordum beðeahte,
hwealfum lindum, þa ðe hwile ær
215 elþeodigra edwit þoledon,
hæðenra hosp. Him þæt hearde wearð
æt ðam æscplegan eallum forgolden
Assyrium, syððan Ebreas
under guðfanum gegan hæfdon
220 to ðam fyrdwicum. Hie ða fromlice
leton forð fleogan flana scuras, |
(hilde)nædran of hornbogan,   [207ᵇ]
strælas st(edehea)rde. Styrmdon hlude
grame guðfreca(n), garas sendon
225 in heardra gemang. Hæleð wæro(n) (y)rre,
landbuende laðum cynne,
stopon styrnmode, stercedferhðe
wrehton unsofte ealdgeniðlan
medowerige. Mundum brugdon
230 scealcas of sceaðum scirmæled swyrd
ecgum gecoste, slogon eornoste
Assiria oretmæcgas,
niðhycgende, nanne ne sparedon
þæs herefolces, hea⟨n⟩e ne rice

(213) beðeahte: Thwaites bedeahte.
(234) MS heanne. D. heane.

---

(219) guðfanum: cf modern English gonfanon, later form gonfalon
(NED).

(222) hornbogan: cf Beow 2437 and see Klaeber's Glossary.

(228) wrehton: 'aroused', occurs also at 243, and Elene 106 and
Psalm 145, 7. Cook cites Daniel 576, but wreceð is from a different verb.

(234) hea⟨n⟩e: MS heanne. If this is allowed to stand, rice should be
altered into ricne acc.sing.; so Cook. But it seems more likely, on
account of the following ne and the many n's in the neighbourhood,
that the scribe put one n too many in heanne than that he should have
left one out in rice: nanne, like modern English none, has a plural
connotation.   28

235 cwicera manna   þe hie ofercuman mihton.
    Swa ða magoþegnas   on ða morgentíd   XII.
    ehton elðeoda   ealle þrage,
    oð þæt ongeaton   ða ðe grame wæron,
    ðæs herefolces   heafodweardas,
240 þæt him swyrdgeswing   swiðlic eowdon
    weras Ebrisce.   Hie wordum þæt
    þam yldestan   ealdorþegnum
    cyðan eodon,   wrehton cumbolwigan
    7 him forhtlice   færspel bodedon
245 medowerigum   morgencollan,
    atolne ecgplegan.   þa ic ædre gefrægn
    slegefæge hæleð | slæpe tobredon   [208ª
    7 wið þæs bealofullan   burgeteldes
    weras ⟨werig⟩ferhðe   hwearfum þringan
250 Ho(lo)fernus.   Hogedon aninga
    hyra hlaforde   ⟨hilde⟩ bodian,
    ærðonðe him se egesa   onufan sæte
    mægen Ebrea.   Mynton ealle
    þæt se beorna brego   7 seo beorhte mægð
255 in ðam wlitegan træfe   wæron ætsomne,
    Iudith seo æðele   7 se galmoda,

(239) heafod-: Thwaites heofod.
(241) ebrisce: Thwaites Ebreisce.
(248) Junius read an accent, which is now illegible, on bur.
(249) MS ferhðe. Grein werig- instead of weras; Sweet hreowig-.
D. follows Grein. þringan: Junius, Thwaites bringan.
(251) MS hyldo.

---

(244) færspel bodedon: cf the same expression Juliana 276.
(246) ic ædre gefrægn, etc: as to the place of ædre, see Klaeber's note
to Beow 575; Hoops, Beowulf Kommentar 74 note.
(247) tobredon: see 150. The expression slæpe tobredan also occurs
in Genesis 2666 and Andreas 1527.
(249) ⟨werig⟩ ferhðe: MS ferhðe, but an alliterating word is re-
quired, and werigferhðe occurs at 290. Cf Daniel 406 gewurðad
[wide]ferhð.
(251) ⟨hilde⟩: MS hyldo, evidently as a result of religious associa-
tion on the part of the scribe. For other examples of religious associa-
tion, see Sisam, RES xxii, 268 note (=Sisam, p. 43, note).
(256) galmoda: cf galferhð 62 and see Introduction p. 11.

egesfull 7 afor.   Næs ðeah eorla nán
þe ðone wiggend   aweccan dorste
oððe gecunnian   hu ðone cumbolwigan
260 wið ða halgan mægð   hæfde geworden,
Metodes meowlan.   Mægen nealæhte,
folc Ebrea,   fuhton þearle
heardum heoruwæpnum,   hæ⟨s⟩te guldon
hyra fyrngeflitu   fagum swyrdum
265 ealde æfðoncan.   Assyria wearð
on ðam dægweorce   dom geswiðrod,
bælc forbiged.   Beornas stodon
ymbe hyra þeodnes træf   þearle gebylde,
sweorcendferhðe.   Hi ða somod ealle
270 ongunnon cohhetan,   cirman hlude
7 gristbitian   gode orfeorme,

(263) MS *hæfte*, so D.
(266) MS *dæge weorce*.
(268) MS full stop after *træf*.

---

(257) *afor*: in poetry the word occurs only here and in *Guthlac* 519.

(260) *geworden*: the examples of *geweorðan*, impersonally constructed with acc., mentioned in Grein-Köhler, are different in meaning. Here the meaning is 'to fare', as in the *Later Genesis* 387; cf Introduction p. 14.

(263) *hæ⟨s⟩te*: MS *hæfte*. The reading *hæste* was first suggested by Grein and accepted by Sweet and Cook, who took it as an adverb. Grein-Köhler give it under the noun *hæst*, Gothic *haifsts* 'violence', cf *Genesis* 1396. BT takes it under *hæft* 'haft', *pars pro toto* for 'sword' (cf *ord*, *ecg*) and translates 'fought with the haft (=sword)', but BTSu remarks: 'In *Jud* 263 perhaps *hæste* should be read.' As it is more likely that a variant of the adv. *ðearle* (262) is meant here than that the instrumental sing. *hæfte* should vary the dat.plural *fagum swyrdum* (264), the reading *hæste* adv. is preferred in the sense 'vehemently'.

(266) *dægweorce*: MS *dæge weorce*. The scribe wrote word by word and inflected *dæg*, just as in the MS reading *eaxle ge spanne* in *Dream of the Rood* 9.

(267) *bælc*: see Introduction p. 5.

(270) *cohhetan*: the meaning is really 'to cough'. Cook's 'lament (?), wail (?)' and BT's 'bluster' do not do justice to the poet's irony; see p. 13.

(271) *gode orfeorme*; cf *Andreas* 406 *gōde orfeorme* (=1617). As the

míd toðon torn þoligende.   þa wæs hyra tires æt ende,|
(ea)des 7 ellendæda.   Hogedon þa eorlas
                      awecc(an)   [208ᵇ]
(hy)ra winedryhten: him wiht ne speow.
275 Þa wear(ð) sið 7 late   sum to ðam arod
    þara beadorinca,   (þæt) he in þæt búrgeteld
    niðheard neðde,   swa hyne nyd fordráf.
    Funde ða on bedde   blacne lic(gan)
    his goldgifan   gæstes gesne,
280 lifes belidenne.   He þa lungre gefeoll
    freorig to foldan,   ongan his feax teran
    hreoh on mode   7 his hrægl somod
    7 þæt word acwæð   to ðam wiggendum
    þe ðær unrote   ute wæron:
285 "Her ys geswutelod   ure sylfra forwyrd,
    toweard getacnod,   þæt þære tide ys
    mid niðum neah geðrungen,   þe (we) sculon ⟨nu⟩losian,
    somod æt sæcce forweorðan.   Her lið sweorde geheawen,
    beheafdod healde(nd) ure."   Hi ða hreowigmode
290 wurpon   hyra wæpe(n) ofdune,   gewitan him werig-
         ferhðe

(287) *nu* not in MS, D. *nyde.*

---

poet more often copies half-lines from other poems, it seems prefer-
able to read *gōde* here, not *Gode*, as Cook does.

(272) *tires æt ende*: Sweet explains this as a confusion of two con-
structions: *þa wæs hyra tir æt ende* and *þa wæs hyra tires ende*, but the
expression occurs more often in Old English (*Judgment Day I* 2 *feores
bið æt ende anra gehwylcum; Beow* 224 *þa wæs sund liden, eoletes æt
ende*). The genitives are perhaps semi-adverbial.

(272) The arrangement is according to Pope 100.

(279) Strictly speaking, the acc. of the adj. ought to be *gesnne.*

(287) Impersonal construction, as is common with 'approach' in
expressions of time, e.g. *nealæcan* + dative. Some word with *n* is
necessary to restore the alliteration. The arrangement is as proposed
in Kluge's *Lesebuch.*

(287) MS *þe/sculon.* Junius and Thwaites read *þe we.*

(289) *hreowigmode*: cf Introduction p. 11.

(290) *gewitan . . . sceacan: gewitan,* 3pl.pret.ind., with late *-an* for
-on. Gewitan is frequently followed by a verb of motion, see Klaeber,
glossary s.v. *gewitan. Him* is added pleonastically to verbs of motion
(and of rest), as in *Beow* 26, 234, etc.

JUDITH

on fleam sceacan.   Him mon feaht on last,
mægeneacen folc,   oð se mæsta dæl
þæs heriges læg   hilde gesæged
on ðam sigewonge,   sweordum geheawen,
295 wulfum to willan   7 eac wælgifrum
fuglum to | frofre.   Flugon ða ðe lyfdo(n)   [209ª
laðra lind(e),   him on laste for
sweot Ebrea   sigore geweorðod,
dom(e) gedyrsod.   Him feng Dryhten God
300 fægre on fultum,   Frea ælmihtig.
Hi ða fromlice   fagum swyrdum
hæleð higerofe   herpað worhton
þurh laðra gemong,   linde heowon,
scildburh scær(on).   Sceotend wæron
305 guðe gegremede,   guman Ebrisce,
þegnas on ða tíd   þearle gelyste
gárgewinnes.   Þær on greot gefeoll
se hyhsta dæl   heafodgerimes,
Assiria   ealdorduguðe,

(292) *eacen*—with *a* inserted above the line in the same hand.
(297) There is one letter very vaguely visible after *lind*. Junius,
Thwaites: *lind*; so also Sweet.
(298) *sigore* added above the line in the same hand.
(305) Thwaites *Ebreisce*.
(306) full stop after *gelyste* in MS.

---

(291) *him mon feaht on last*: cf *on last faran* in *Beow* 2945; *on laste
hwearf* in *Finnsburh* 17, etc, and below 297 (*him on laste for*) and 209.
(297) *linde*: The stroke still visible after *lind* in the manuscript is
probably that of an *e*. If we read *linde*, the half-line remains normal.
With the emendation *lindwiggendra* (Ettmüller, Grein, Cook) it be-
comes hypermetrical in normal surroundings. D. *lindwerod*.
(302) *herpað*: cf *Daniel* 38 *herepað*. The word is common in charters,
see examples in BT. For *a* instead of *æ*, see SB 49, note 2, and cf
siðfate 336.
(304) *scildburh*: cf Cook's note to this line. The habit of forming a
scildburh is attested by Caesar (*De Bello Gallico* I. 52) and other early
historians. In Old English poetry examples are found in *Beow* 3118
(*scildweall*), *Elene* 652 (*bordhaga*), *Maldon* 102 (*wihagan*), 242 (*scild-
burh*), 277 (*bordweall*), *Brunanburh* 5 (*bordweall*).
(308) *se hyhsta dæl*: 'the greater part'. Other examples in BTSu s.v.
heah.

32

310 laðan cynnes. Lythwón becóm
    cwicera to cyððe. Cirdon cynerofe,
    wiggend on wiðertrod, wælscel oninnan,
    reocende hrǽw. Rúm wæs to nimanne
    londbuendum on ðam laðestan,
315 hyra ealdfeondum unlyfigendum
    heolfrig hereréaf, hyrsta scyne,
    bord 7 brad swyrd, brune helmas,
    dyre madmas. Hæfdon dómlice
    on ðam folcstede fynd oferwunnen
320 eðelweardas, ealdhettende
    swyrdum aswefede. Hie on swaðe reston,
    þa ðe him to life laðost wæron |
    (cw)icera cynna. (Þ)a seo cneoris eall,   [209^b]
    mægða (m)ærost, anes monðes fyrst,
325 wlanc wundenlocc (w)ægon 7 læddon
    to ðære beorhtan byrig Bethuliam
    helmas 7 hupseax, hare byrnan,
    guðsceorp gumena golde gefrætewod,
    mærra madma ⟨ma⟩þonne mon ænig
330 asecgan mæge sear(o)þoncelra.
    Eal þæt ða ðeodguman þrymme geeodon

(312) full stop after *wiðertrod* in MS.
(317) D. *bradswyrd*.
(319) *fynd*: Junius, Thwaites *fyrd*.
(322) full stop after *wæron* in MS.
(325) *wundenlocc*: Junius, Thwaites *wundenloce*. (*w*)*ægon*: Junius,
Thwaites *wagon*, but the loop of the *æ* is just visible. D. *wagon*.
(329) *ma* not in MS.

---

(313) *rum*: 'opportunity', as in *Beow* 2690.
(319) *folcstede*: 'battle-field' is not the usual meaning of the word,
but this meaning occurs more often, see BTSu s.v. *folcstede*.
(325) (*w*)*ægon*: the *æ* is still visible in the manuscript. Junius and
Thwaites read *ā*.
(327) *hare byrnan*: this half-line is probably taken from *Beow* 2153;
cf also *Waldere* II.17. The sense 'grey' seems best, not 'hoary' or 'ancient'.
(329) *mærra madma⟨ma⟩*: it is possible that the scribe skipped *ma*
owing to the last syllable of *madma*; or *māre mādma* as Mossé reads.
Another possibility is *mærran madmas*, also suggested by Mossé 414.
(331) *geeodon*: cf note to 122.

cene under cumblu*m* ⟨on⟩ compwige
þurh Iudithe   gleawe lare
mægð modigre.   Hi to mede hyre
335 of ða*m* siðfate   sylfre brohton
eorlas æscrofe   Holofernes
sweord 7 swatigne helm,   swylce eac side (by)rnan,
gerenode readu*m* golde,   7 eal þæt se rinca bal*d*or
swiðmod sinces ahte   oððe sundoryrfes,
340 beaga 7 beorhtra maðma,   hi þæt þære beorhtan idese
ageafon gearoþoncolre.   Ealles ðæs Iudith sægde
wuldor weroda Dryhtne,   þe hyre weorðmynde   geaf,
mærðe on moldan rice,   swylce eac mede on heofonu*m*,
sigorlean(in swegles)wuldre, þæs ðe heo ahte soðne geleafan
345 a to ða(m) Ælmihtigan.   Huru æt ðam ende ne tweode
þæs lea(nes) þe heo la)nge gyrnde.   Þæs sy ða*m* leofan
    Dryhtne
wu(ldor) to widan aldre,   þe gesceop wind 7 lyfte,
roderas 7 rume grundas,   swylce eac reðe streamas
7 swe(g)l(es d)reamas   þ(ur)h his syl(fes miltse).

(332) MS 7.

(335) *sylfre*: Junius, Thwaites *sylfne*.

(336) Thwaites *Holofernes*.

(344) full stop after *ahte* in MS.

(345) *a* not in MS; full stop after *ælmihtigan*, after *huru* and after
tweode in MS.

(346) full stop after *gyrnde* in MS.

(347) full stop after *aldre* in MS.

(348) full stop after *grundas* in MS.

---

(332) ⟨*on*⟩: MS 7 *compwige*; so also Junius and Thwaites. It is
possible that *on* was skipped by the scribe, although the sense is
better if we keep *on*.

(335) *siðfate*: cf note to 302.

(342) The expression *wuldor secgean* does not occur elsewhere. The
meaning is presumably 'for all this Judith ascribed glory to God', i.e.
gave thanks in glory to God.

(344) From *in swegles* to the end the lines are copied from the
Junuis MS in an early modern hand. See Sisam, p. 2.

(345) *a* has been supplied in conformity with l. 7a.

(349) There is no justification for Pope's reading *sæs* and *swegles
dreamas* (130 note 16). Type A with anacrusis is admittedly rare, but
may be accepted together with the other metrical irregularities of
Judith.

BIBLIOGRAPHY

1. MANUSCRIPT, TRANSCRIPTION

British Museum, MS Cotton Vitellius A XV.
Bodley Library, MS Junius 105.
Wanley in Hickes's *Thesaurus* II. 219.

2. EDITIONS

1698 E. Thwaites, *Heptateuchus, Liber Job et Evangelium Nicodemi; Anglo Saxonice. Historiae Judith Fragmentum; Dano-Saxonice.*

1834 B. Thorpe, *Analecta Anglo-Saxonica.* New ed., with corrections, 1846.

1835 L. Ettmüller, *Engla and Seaxna Scopas and Boceras.*

1838 H. Leo, *Altsächsische und Angelsächsische Sprachproben.*

1849 L. F. Klipstein, *Analecta Anglo-Saxonica* II. 15–350; 1–14 in the Notes.

1857 C. W. M. Grein, *Bibliothek der Angelsächsischen Poesie,* 2nd ed. by Wülcker, II (1894).

1858 L. G. Nilsson, *Judith* (with a translation in Swedish).

1861 M. Rieger, *Alt- und Angelsächsisches Lesebuch.*

1876 H. Sweet, *An Anglo-Saxon Reader,* 12th ed. 1950.

1880 K. Körner, *Einleitung in das Studium des Angelsächsischen,* Part II.

1882 J. Zupitza, *Alt- und Mittelenglisches Übungsbuch,* 10th ed. 1912 (ll. 122–235).

1888 A. S. Cook, *Judith: An Old English Epic Fragment,* 2nd ed. 1889.

1888 F. Kluge, *Angelsächsisches Lesebuch,* 3rd ed. 1902.

1904 A. S. Cook, *Judith* (Belles Lettres Series).

1919 A. J. Wyatt, *An Anglo-Saxon Reader.*

1945 F. Mossé, *Manuel de l'Anglais du Moyen Age,* I. Vieil-Anglais (ll. 159–350).

1954 E. Van Kirk Dobbie, *Beowulf and Judith* (The Anglo-Saxon Poetic Records, Vol. IV).

1970 R. Hamer, *A Choice of Anglo-Saxon Verse.*

1974 O. Funke and K. Jost, *An Old English Reader,* 6th ed. (ll. 15-121).

3. TRANSLATIONS

1858 L. G. Nilsson, see above under 2.

1887 H. Morley, *English Writers,* II.

1888 A. S. Cook, see above under 2.

35

JUDITH

1889 E. H. Hickey, *Journal of Education*, New Series xi (ll. 1-121).
1889 J. M. Garnett, *Elene, Judith, Athelstan . . . , Byrhtnoth . . . , and the Dream of the Rood*, 2nd ed. 1901.
1901 O. Elton, *An English Miscellany presented to Dr. F. J. Furnivall* (ll. 1-121).
1902 J. L. Hall, *Judith, Phoenix and other Anglo-Saxon Poems*.
1926 R. K. Gordon, *Anglo-Saxon Poetry*, Everyman's Library, 2nd ed. 1950.
1970 R. Hamer, see above under 2.

4. CRITICISMS, STUDIES, ETC

1889 A. S. Cook, 'Notes on a Northumbrianised Version of Judith', in *Transactions of the American Philological Association* xx 172–174.
1892 T. Gregory Foster, *Judith, Studies in Metre, Language and Style*, Quellen und Forschungen 71.
1892 A. Müller, *Der syntaktische gebrauch des verbums in dem ags. gedichte von der Judith*.
1892 M. Neumann, *Über das altenglische Gedicht von Judith*.
1898 F. Brinckner, *Germanische Altertümer in dem angelsächsischen Gedicht Judith*.
1903 A. S. Cook, 'Notes on Judith', *JEGP* v 153-8.
1905 M. W. Smyth, 'The numbers in the manuscript of the Old English Judith', *MLN* xx 197-9.
1907 K. Oldenburg, *Untersuchungen über die syntax in dem altenglischen gedicht Judith*.
1908 A. Brandl, in Paul's *Grundriss der germanischen Philologie* II, 1091.
1912 F. Tupper, 'Notes on Old English poems I: the home of the Judith', *JEGP* xi 82-9.
1927 E. Purdie, *The Story of Judith in German and English Literature*.
1943 C. W. Kennedy, *The Earliest English Poetry*.
1948 Kemp Malone, in A. C. Baugh, *A Literary History of England*, Book I, Part I.
1953 K. Sisam, *Studies in the History of Old English Literature*.
1955 R. E. Woolf, 'The Lost Opening to the "Judith" ', *MLR* 168-72.
1961 K. Malone, 'Some Judith readings', *Festschrift zum 75 Geburtstag von T. Spira*, pp. 32-7.
1962 A. Renoir, 'Judith and the limits of poetry', *ES* xliii 145-55.
1964 C. Enzensberger, 'Das altenglische Judith-Gedicht als Stilgebilde', *Anglia* lxxxii 433-57.
1967 D. K. Fry, 'The heroine on the beach in Judith', *NM* lxviii 168-84.
1968 A. G. Brodeur, 'A study of diction and style in three Anglo-Saxon narrative poems', *Nordica et Anglica' studies in honor of S. Einarsson*, pp. 97-114.

BIBLIOGRAPHY

1968 D. K. Fry, 'Imagery and a point of view in Judith 206-31', ELN
v 157-9.

1970 F. J. Heinemann, 'Judith 236-291a: a mock heroic approach-to-
battle type scene', NM lxxi 83-96.

1970 B. F. Huppé, The Web of Words, pp. 114-89.

1971 J. J. Campbell, 'Schematic technique in Judith', ELH xxxviii 155-
72.

1971 J. F. Doubleday, 'The principle of contrast in Judith', NM lxxii
436-41.

1971 D. K. Fry, 'Type-scene composition in Judith', Annuale Mediæ-
vale xii 100-19.

1973 K. T. Berkhout and J. F. Doubleday, 'The net in Judith 46b-54a',
NM lxxiv 238-46.

1973 J. Mushabac, 'Judith and the theme of Sapientia et Fortitudo',
Massachusetts Studies in English, iv 3-12.

1975 D. Chamberlain, 'Judith: a fragmentary and political poem', L.E.
Nicholson and D. W. Frese, ed., Anglo-Saxon Poetry: Essays in
Appreciation, pp. 135-59.

1975 I. Pringle, 'Judith: the homily and the poem', Traditio xxxi 83-97.

1975 B. Raffel, 'Judith: hypermetricity and rhetoric', Nicholson and
Frese op. cit., pp. 124-34.

5. METRE

1886 K. Luick, 'Uber den Versbau des Angelsächsischen Gedichtes
Judith', in Paul und Braune's Beiträge xi, 470–492.

1893 E. Sievers, Altgermanische Metrik.

1942 J. C. Pope, The Rhythm of Beowulf.

GLOSSARY

In the Glossary words will be found under the forms in which they occur, except that nouns and adjectives (excluding irregular comparatives, &c) will be found under the nom.sg. (masc.) and verbs under the infinitive (except that the present forms of 'to be' will be found under *beon*, the pret. forms under *wesan*); pronouns under the nom.sg.masc. (except the 1st and 2nd pers. of the personal pronouns which will be found under the nom.sg. or the nom.pl. as the case may be). When the reference is followed by * it indicates a restored or emended form and when followed by n it is a reference to the appropriate note. The order of letters is alphabetical. *þ, ð* follows *t*. The OE characters, *ę, ȝ, ƿ* are replaced by *æ, g, w*. The prefix *ge-* is always ignored in the arrangement of the glossary. For abbreviations see *Deor* (ed. Kemp Malone) p. 32 or *Waldere* (ed. F. Norman), p. 49.

A

ā, *adv.*, always, ever, 7.

ābregdan, *v.(3),* [ABRAID]; draw 79.

ac, *conj.*, [AC]; but 60, 119 *etc* and 209.

ācweðan, *v.(5),* [AQUEATH]; speak 82, 151, 283.

āfor, *adj.*, fierce 257.

āgan, āhte *(pret.)* 3, 6, 344; *(pret.pres.),* [OWE]; have, possess, 196; *w.neg.,* **nāhte** 91.

āgēotan, agotene *(p.part.)* 32n; *v.(2),* [AGETEN]; deprive of.

āgiefan, āgeaf *(pret.sg.)* 130, **āgēafon** *(pret.pl.)* 341; *v.(5),* [AGIVE]; give.

āhōn, āhongen *(p.part.)* 48; *v.(7),* [AHANG]; hang.

aldor, *m.a-stem,* [ALDER *sb.²*], see **ealdor.**

aldre, *d.sg.,* see **ealdor,** *n.*

ālecgan, ālēde *(pret.)* 101, [ALLAY *v.¹*]; lay, place.

alwalda, *m.n-stem,* GOD, the Almighty, 84.

ān, *num.,* ONE 64, 95, 324.

anbyhtscealc, *m.a-stem,* [+ SHALK]; retainer 38.

and, *conj.*, AND 8 *etc.* (MS only 7).

āninga, *adv.*, at once, forthwith, 250.

ārētan, *w.v.(1),* cheer, gladden, 167 *(p.part.).*

ārfæst, *adj.*, [ORE + FAST]; glorious 190.

arod, *adj.*, bold 275.

āsecgan, *w.v.(3),* relate 330.

Assirias, *n.pl.,* Assyrians 232, 265, 309 *(gen.pl.);* 218 *(d.pl.).*

āswebban, āswefede *(p.part. pl.)* 321; *w.v.(1),* [ASWEVE]; put to death, destroy.

atol, *adj.*, [ATEL; *used as a n.*, the terrible one 75; terrible 246 *(acc.sg.).*

āwa, *adv.*, always, ever, 120.

38

āweccan, w.v.(1), [AWECCHE]; awake 258, 274.

ǣdre, adv., forthwith 64, 95, 246.

ǣfre, adv., EVER 114.

æfter, prep.w.dat., along 18; AFTER 117; adv., after, towards, 65n.

æfðonca, m.n-stem, grudge 265.

ǣghwylc, pron., each 50, 166.

ælfscīne, adj., beautiful as an elf 14n.

ælmihtig, adj., ALMIGHTY 300; the Almighty 7, 345.

ǣnig, pron., ANY 329.

ǣr, adv., before 65, 143, 214; conj., ERE, before, 76; ǣrest, sup., first 14.

ǣrðonðe, conj., before 252.

æscplega, m.n-stem, [ASH sb.¹ + PLAY sb.]; spear-play, battle, 217.

æscrōf, adj., brave 336.

æt, prep.w.dat., from 3; in 123, 175, 197, 217, 288; AT 272, 345.

ǣt, n.a-stem. [EAT, sb.]; food, prey, 210.

ætsomne, adv., together 255.

ætȳwan, w.v.(1), [ATEW]; display 174.

æðele, adj., [ATHEL, a.]; noble 176, 256.

B

baldor, m.a-stem, lord, king, 9, 49 etc.

bælc, m.i-stem, pride 267.

gebǣran, w.v.(1), [I-BERE]; cry out in joy 27n.

be, prep.w.dat., [cf BY]; by 81, 99.

beadorinc, m.a-stem, warrior 276.

beadu, f.wō-stem, battle 175, 213.

beæftan, adv., [BAFT]; behind 112.

bēag, m.a-stem, [BEE²]; ring, bracelet, 36, 340.

bēahhroden, adj., adorned with rings 138 (nom.pl.).

beald, adj., BOLD 17.

bealofull, adj., BALEFUL, wicked, 48, 63, 100, 248.

bearhtm, m.a-stem, tumult 39 (instr.).

bearn, n.a-stem., [BAIRN]; child 24, 33 etc.

bebēodan, v.(2), [BIBEDE]; command 38, 144.

becuman, v.(4), [BECOME]; arrive 134, 311.

bed, n.ja-stem, BED 48, 63, 72 etc.

bedrest, f.jō-stem, bed 36.

bēgen, bēgea (gen.pl.) 128, bā (n.pl.f.) 133; num., [BO]; both 207.

behēafdian, behēafdod (p. part.) 289; w.v.(2), BEHEAD.

bēhð, f.ō-stem, sign, proof, 174.

belīðan, belidenne (p.part.) 280; v.(1), deprive of.

benǣman, w.v.(1), [BENEME]; deprive of 76.

benc, f.i-stem, BENCH 18.

bencsittend, m.nd-stem, bench-sitter, guest, 27.

bēon, anom.v., BE; ys (3p.sg.) 86, 87 etc; sȳ (3p.sg.subj.) 346; syndon (pl.) 195.

beorht, adj., BRIGHT, fair, 58, 254 etc.

beorn, m.a-stem, [BERNE]; man, hero, 213, 267; 254 (gen.pl.).

beran, boren (p.part.) 18; v.(4), BEAR; carry 131, 191, 201.

besmītan, v.(1), [BESMIT]; defile, pollute, 59.

Bethulia, Bethulia 138 (acc.sg.), 326.

beðeccan, beðeahte (p.part.) 213, w.v.(1), [+ THATCH], cover, protect.

39

bewindan, *v.*(*3*), [BEWIND]; surround 115.

bīdan, gebidenne (*p.part.*) 64; *v.*(*1*), BIDE; attain 64.

biddan, *v.*(*5*), BID, ask, request, 84, 187.

bindan, *v.*(*3*), BIND 115.

binnan, *adv.*, [BIN]; within 64.

blāc, *adj.*, [BLAKE, cf BLOKE], pale 278.

blāchlēor, *adj.*, with pale cheeks 128.

blǣd, *m.a-stem*, [BLEAD]; period of flourishing, prosperity, fame, 63; glory 122.

blīcan, *v.*(*1*), [BLIK]; glitter 137.

blīðe, *adj.*, BLITHE, joyous, 58, 159; graciously minded 154.

blōdig, *adj.*, BLOODY 126, 174.

blondan, geblonden (*p.part.*)34; *v.*(*7*), [BLAND¹]; mix, confuse.

bodian, *w.v.*(*2*), BODE, announce, 244, 251.

bolla, *m.n-stem*, BOWL; cup 17.

bord, *n.a-stem*, [BOARD]; shield 192, 317 (*acc.pl.*); 213 (*dat.pl.*).

brād, *adj.*, BROAD 317.

bregdan, *v.*(*3*),[BRAID];draw 229.

brego, *m.u-stem*, ruler, prince, 39, 254.

brēme, *adj.*, [BREME];famous 57.

brēost, *n.a-stem*, BREAST 192.

bringan, *w.v.* (1), bring, 335 (*pret.pl.*).

gebringan, gebrōhte (*pret.sg.*) 125; *w.v.*(*1*) + BRING, conduct 54 (*pret.pl.*); 57 (*p.part.*).

brōga, *m.n-stem*, terror 4 (*gen. sg.*).

brūn, *adj.*, BROWN; shining 317.

brytta, *m.n-stem*, distributor, lord, 30, 90, 93 *etc.*

būne, *f.n-stem*, cup 18.

burg, *f.monos.-stem.*, [BOROUGH]; city, fortress, 58 *etc*, 137 (*gen.sg.*).

būrgeteld, *n.a-stem.*, [BOWER + TELD];pavilion,tent,57,248,276.

burhlēode, *m.i-stem*, citizen 175 (*dat.pl.*).

burhsittend, *m.nd-stem*, citizen 159.

būtan, *prep.w.dat.*, [BOUT]; without 120.

byldan, gebylde (*p.part.*), [BIELD]; excite 268.

byrne, *f.n-stem*, [BURNE]; corslet 322, 337.

byrnhom, *m.a-stem*, corslet 192.

byrnwiga, *m.a-stem*, corsleted warrior, 39.

byrnwiggend, *m.nd-stem*, corsleted warrior 17.

bysmerlīce, *adv.*, [cf BISMER]; shamefully 100.

C

camp, *m.a-stem*, [CAMP¹]; fight 200.

cēne, *adj.*, KEEN; brave 200, 332.

cirman, *w.v.*(*1*), [CHIRM]; cry out, shriek, 270.

cirran, *w.v.*(*1*), [CHARE *v.*]; turn back 311.

cnēoris, *f.jō-stem*, tribe, nation, 323.

cohhetan, *w.v.*(*1*), [cf COUGH]; to make a noise 270n.

collenferhð, *adj.*, bold, elated, 134.

compwīg, *n.a-stem*, battle 332.

gecost, *adj.*, tried, excellent, 231.

cuman, *v.*(*4*), COME 11 (*pret.pl.*); *pret.sg.* 50; *cumen* (*p.part.*) 146, 168.

cumbol, *n.a-stem*, standard, banner, 332.

cumbolwiga, *m.a-stem*, warrior 243, 259.

gecunnian, *w.v.*(*2*), [CUN]; investigate, inquire, 259.

cwic, *adj.*, QUICK; living 235, 311, 323.

cynerōf, *adj.*, brave, noble, 200, 311.

cyning, *m.a-stem*, KING 190; 155 (*gen.pl.*).

cynn, *n.ja-stem*, KIN; race, people, 52, 310 (*gen.sg.*); (*dat. sg.*) 226; (*gen.pl.*) 323.

cȳðan, *w.v.(1)*, [KITHE]; announce 56, 243. *gecȳðed* (*p. part.*) 155.

cȳðð(u), *f.ō-stem*, KITH; native land 311.

D

dæg, *m.a-stem*, DAY 28.

dægred, *n.a-stem*, [DAYRED]; dawn 204.

dægweorc, *n.a-stem*, DAYWORK 266.

dǣl, *m.i-stem*, DEAL; part 292, 308.

dēad, *adj.*, DEAD 107.

dear, dorste (*pret.*) 258, *pret. pres.(3)*, DARE.

deað, *m.a-stem*, DEATH 31.

dēma, *m.n-stem*, judge 4 (*gen.sg.*), 59, 94.

dēman, *w.v.(1)*, DEEM; condemn 196.

dēofolcund, *adj.*, [DEVIL +]; diabolical 61.

dōgor, *n.os/es-stem*, day 12 (*instr.*).

dolhwund, *adj.*, wounded 107.

dōm, *m.a-stem*, DOOM; glory 196, 266, 299.

dōmlīce, *adv.*, gloriously 318.

dōn, *anom.v.*, DO 95.

drēam, *m.a-stem*, [DREAM¹]; joy 349.

drēfan, gedrēfed (*p.part.*) 88; *w.v.(1)*; [DREVE]; afflict.

drencan, *w.v.(1)*, DRENCH 29.

drēogan, *v.(2)*, DREE, suffer, 158 (*pret.*).

druncen, *adj.* (*p.part.*), DRUN-KEN 67, 107.

dryhten, *m.a-stem*, [DRIGHTIN]; Lord, God, 61, 92 *etc*; Lord, King, 21.

dryhtguma, *m.n-stem*, retainer 29.

duguð, *f.ō-stem*, [DOUTH]; host 31 (*acc.sg.*), 61 (*gen.pl.*).

dynian, *w.v.(2)*, DIN; clamour 23; clash 204.

dȳre, *adj.*, DEAR, precious, 318.

dȳrsian, *w.v.(2)*, glorify 299.

E

ēac, *adv.*, EKE, also, 18, 295 *etc.*

ēad, *n.a-stem*, success 273.

ēadhrēðig, *adj.*, triumphant 135.

ēadig, *adj.*, [EADI]; blessed 35.

eald, *adj.*, [ELD a.]; OLD 166, 265; *sup. yldesta*, 10, 242.

ealdfēond, *m.nd-stem*, ancient foe 315.

ealdgenīðla, *m.n-stem*, ancient enemy 228.

ealdhettend, *m.nd-stem*, ancient enemy 320.

ealdor, *m.a-stem*, [ALDER]; prince 38, 58 *etc.*

ealdor, *n.a-stem*, life 76, 185. *aldre* (*dat.sg.*) 120, 347; *awa to aldre* and *to widan aldre*, for ever and ever, 120, 347.

ealdorduguð, *f.ō-stem*, nobility, leaders, 309.

ealdorþegn, *m.a-stem*, cf THANE; chief retainer 242.

eall, *adj.*, ALL 8, 10, 16 *etc.* *ealles* (*adv.gen.*), entirely 108.

eallgylden, *adj.*, [ALL + GOL-DEN], allgolden 46.

earn, *m.a-stem*, [ERNE]; eagle 210.

41

ēastan, *adv.,* [EAST]; from the east 190.

ēaðe, *adv.,* [EATH]; easily; *sup.* **ēaðost** 75, 102.

ēaðmēdu, *f.ō-stem,* [EDMEDE *sb.*]; reverence 170 (*dat.pl.*).

Ebrēas, *m.pl.,* Hebrews 218, 253, 262, 298.

Ebrisc, *adj.,* Hebrew 241, 305.

ecg, *f.jō-stem,* EDGE 231.

ecgplega, *m.n-stem,* EDGE + PLAY; battle 246.

edwīt, *n.a-stem,* [EDWIT]; insolence 215.

eft, *adv.,* [EFT]; back, again, 146, 169.

egesa, *m.n-stem,* terror 252.

egesful, *adj.,* [cf AWFUL]; terrible 21, 257.

eglan, *w.v.*(1), AIL; trouble, plague, 185.

ēhtan, *w.v.*(1), pursue 237 (*pret. pl.*).

ellen, *n.a-stem,* ELNE; courage 95.

ellendǣd, *f.i-stem,* DEED of courage 273.

ellenrōf, *adj.,* brave, courageous, 109, 146.

ellenþrīste, *adj.,* courageous 133.

ellor, *adv.,* elsewhere 112.

elðēod, *f.ō-stem,* [cf THEDE]; foreign people 237.

elðēodig, *adj.,* [ALTHEODI]; foreign 215.

ende, *m.ja-stem,* END 64, 120 *etc.*

ēode, *pret.,* went 15 (*pret.pl.*), 55 *etc.* See **gān.**

geēodon, see **gegān.**

eorl, *m.a-stem,* [EARL]; man, hero, 21, 257 *etc.*

eornoste, *adv.,* [EARNEST *adv.*]; vehemently 108, 231.

eorðe, *f.n-stem,* EARTH 65.

ēow, see **gē.**

ēowan, *w.v.*(1), reveal, make known, 240.

ēower, *poss.pron.,* your 195.

ēðel, *m.a-stem,* [ETHEL]; home 169.

ēðelweard, *m.a-stem,* guardian of the country 320.

F

fæder, *m.r-stem,* FATHER 5.

fǣge, *adj.,* FEY, death-doomed, 19, 195, 209.

fæger, *adj.,* FAIR 47. **fægre,** *adv.,* 300.

fǣrspel, *n.a-stem,* [FEAR *sb.* + SPELL *sb.*[1]]; dreadful tidings 244.

fæste, *adv.,* FAST; firmly 99.

fæsten, *n.ja-stem,* [FASTEN]; stronghold 143.

fæstengeat, *n.a-stem,* castlegate 162.

fætels, *m.a-stem,* [FETLES]; pouch, sack, 127.

fāg, *adj.,* [FAW, *adj.*]; shining 104, 194 *etc.*

faran, *v.*(6), FARE, go, march, 202, 297.

gefeallan, gefēol (*pret.*) 67, 280, 307; *v.*(7), FALL.

feax, *n.a-stem,* [FAX]; hair 99, 281.

gefeoht, *n.a.-stem,* FIGHT, battle, 198, 202.

feohtan, *v.*(3), FIGHT 262, 291.

gefeohtan, *v.*(3), gain by fighting 122.

gefēon, gefeah (*pret.*) 205; *v.*(5), rejoice (*w.gen.*).

fēond, fȳnd (*pl.*), *m.nd.stem,* FIEND, enemy, 195, 319.

fēondsceaða, *m.n-stem,* enemy 104.

feorran, *adv.,* [FERREN]; from afar 24.

42

GLOSSARY

feorða, *adj.num.,* FOURTH 12.
fēran, *w.v.(1),* [FERE]; go, proceed, 12.
ferhōglēaw, *adj.,* wise, prudent, 41.
fetigan, *w.v.(2),* [FET; cf FETCH]; fetch 35.
fēðelāst, *m.a-stem,* [+ LAST]; track, course, 139.
findan, funde *(pret.sg.)* 2, 278; *v.(3),* FIND II, obtain; *fundon (pret.pl.)* 41.
fīras, *m.ja-stem (pl.),* men 24, 33.
flān, *m.a-stem,* [FLANE]; arrow 221.
flēam, *m.a-stem,* [FLEME]; flight 291.
flēogan, flēah *(pret.)* 209; *v.(2),* FLY 221.
flēohnet, *n.ja-stem,* FLYNET, curtain, 47n.
flēon, flugon *(pret.pl.)* 296; *v.(2),* FLEE.
fletsittend, *m.nd-stem,* sitter in hall 19, 33.
flōr, *f.u-stem,* FLOOR 111.
folc, *n.a-stem,* FOLK; people 12, 143, 162 *etc.*
folcstede, *m.i-stem,* battle-field 319.
folctoga, *m.n-stem,* commander 47, 194.
folde, *f.n-stem,* [FOLD sb.¹]; earth 281.
folm, *f.ō-stem,* hand 80, 99.
fōn, fēng *(pret.sg.)* 299; *v.(7),* FANG; *feng on fultum* 299, helped them.
for, *prep.w.dat.,* [FOR]; before 192.
forbīgan, *w.v.(1),* abase 267 *(p.part.).*
forceorfan, *v.(3),* [FORCARVE]; cut through 105.
fordrīfan, fordrāf *(pret.sg.)* 277; *v.(1),* [FORDRIVE]; impel.

foregenga, *m.n-stem,* attendant 127.
foremӕre, *adj.,* illustrious, eminent, 122.
forgifan, *v.(5),* FORGIVE; grant 88.
forgildan, forgolden *(p.part.)* 217; *v.(3),* [FORYIELD]; requite, recompense.
forhtlīce, *adv.,* in fear 244.
forlӕtan, forlēton *(pret.)* 170; *v.(7),* [FORLET]; let 150 *(inf.).*
forlēosan, *v.(2),* [FORLESE]; lose 63.
forð, *adv.,* FORTH 111, 120 *etc.*
forðylman, *w.v.(1),* enwrap, envelop, 118n.
forweorðan, *v.(3),* [FORWORTH]; perish 288.
forwyrd, *f.i-stem,* destruction 285.
frætwan, gefrætewod *(p.part.)* 171, 328; *w.v.(2),* adorn.
frēa, *m.n-stem,* lord 300.
fremman, *w.v.(1),* [FREME]; perform, accomplish, 37.
gefremman, *w.v.(1),* effect 6, 181. *tide gefremede,* 6, "granted".
frēorig, *adj.,* cold, shivering, 281.
gefrignan, *v.(3),* [FRAYNE]; hear, learn, 7, 246.
gefriðian, *w.v.(2),* [FRITH, *v.*²]; protect, defend, 5 *(pret.subj.).*
frōfor, *f.ō-stem,* [FROVER]; consolation, joy, 83, 296.
fromlīce, *adv.,* boldly, promptly, 41.
frumgār, *m.a-stem,* leader, chieftain, 195. (Cf Lat. primi-pilus.)
frymð, *f.ō-stem,* [FRUMTH]; creation 5, 83, 189 *(gen.pl.).*
fugel, *m.a-stem,* FOWL; bird 207, 296.
fūl, *adj.,* FOUL 111.

43

full, *adj.*, FULL 19.

fultum, *m.a-stem*, FULTUM; help 186, 300.

fylgan, *w.v.(1)*, (*orig.(3)*, *w.dat.*, *FOLLOW*; serve 33n.

fyllan, *w.v.(1)*, FELL 194* (*pl. imp.*).

fyllo, *f.in-stem*, FILL, feast, 209.

fyrdwīc, *n.a-stem*, [FERD + WICK *sb.*²]; camp 220.

fyrngeflit, *n.a-stem*, old strife 264 (*acc.pl.*).

fyrst, *m.i-stem*, FRIST; period 324.

fȳsan, *w.v.(1)*, [FUSE]; hasten 189 (*subj.*).

G

gǣst, *m.os/es-stem*, [GHOST]; spirit, life, 83, 112, 279.

gālferhð, *adj.*, [GOLE +]; wanton, licentious, 62.

gālmōd, *adj.*, wanton, licentious, 256.

gān, ēodon (*pret.pl.*) 15, 55 *etc*; *anom.v.*, GO 149.

gār, *m.a-stem*, [GARE]; spear 224.

gārgewinn, *n.i-stem*, battle with spears 307.

gegān, geēodon (*pret.pl.*) 331; *anom.v.*, GO; win. *gegān* (*p. part.*) 140, 219. *geēodon*, they won 331. See gegangan.

gegangan, *v.(7)*, go 64. See gegān.

gē, ēow (*dat.*) 152, 154, 156, 197; ēow (*acc.*) 188; *pron.*, YE 153, 158, 177, 196. See ēower.

ge, *conj.*, [YE]; and, also, 166.

gearo, gearwe (*f.acc.sg.*) 2, [YARE]; ready, prepared.

gearoþoncol, *adj.*, ready-witted 341.

gearwian, gegearewod (*p. part.*) 199; *w.v.(2)*, prepare.

geat, *n.a-stem*, GATE 151.

gegnum, *adv.*, straightaway 132.

geðmor, *adj.*, [YOMER]; sad, troubled, 87.

geðmormōd, *adj.*, sorrowful 144.

geond, *prep.w.acc.*, [YOND]; throughout 156.

geong, *adj.*, YOUNG 166; gingre (*comp.f.*), handmaid 132.

georn, *adj.*, [YERN]; eager, desirous, 210.

georne, *adv.*, eagerly 8.

gēsne, *adj.*, ɩGEASON]; dead 112; deprived 279.

gifan, gēaf (*pret.*) 342; *v.(5)*, GIVE.

gifeðe, *adj.*, granted (by fate) 157.

gifu, *f.ō-stem*, [GIVE *sb.*¹]; gift 2 (*gen.pl.*).

gildan, guldon (*pret.*) 263; *v.(4)*, [YIELD]; requite.

gingre, see geong.

ginn, *adj.*, spacious, wide, 2, 149.

girwan, *w.v.(1)*, provide 9.

glædmōd, *adj.*, [GLAD +]; gladhearted, cheerful, 140.

glēaw, *adj.*, [GLEW *a.*]; prudent, wise, 13, 171, 333.

glēawhȳdig, *adj.*, wise, prudent, 148.

God, *m.a-stem*, GOD 83, 123 *etc*.

gōd, *n.a-stem*, GOOD 32 (*gen.pl.*).

gold, *n.a-stem*, GOLD 171, 328, 338.

goldgifa, *m.n-stem*, gold-giver, lord, 279.

goldwine, *m.i-stem*, [+ WINE *sb.*²]; gold-friend, lord, 22.

gram, *adj.*, [GRAME]; fierce, angry, 224, 238.

gremman, *w.v.(1)*, [GREME]; enrage 305.

grēot, *n.a-stem*, GRIT; sand, earth, 307.

44

grīstbītian, w.v.(2), [GRISTBITE]; to gnash the teeth 271.

grund, m.a-stem, GROUND, earth, 2, 348.

guma, m.n-stem, [GOME]; man 9, 22 etc.

gūð, f.ō-stem, war 123, 305.

gūðfana, m.n-stem, GONFANON, standard, 219n.

gūðfreca, m.n-stem, warrior 224.

gūðsceorp, n.a-stem, armour 328.

gylian, w.v.(1), YELL 25.

gyrnan, w.v.(1), YEARN for 346.

gystern, n.a-stem, [GUEST +]; guest-chamber 40.

gyt, adv., YET 107, 182.

gytesæl, m.f.i-stem, joy at wine-pouring 22 (dat.pl.).

H

habban, hafað (3p.sg.pres.) 197, hæfde (pret.) 64 etc. w.v.(3), HAVE (auxil.).

hālig, adj., HOLY 56, 160 etc.

hām, m.a-stem, HOME 121.

hām, adv., HOME 131.

hand, f.u-stem, HAND 198; hond 130.

hār, adj., HOAR, grey, 328n.

hātan, hēt (pret.) 9, 32, 34, 147, 171; v.(7), [cf HIGHT v.¹]; command. hēte (pret.subj.) 53.

hāte, adv., HOT; hotly, fervidly, 94.

hæftan, w.v.(1), [cf HAFT v.²], bind, imprison, 116.

hæleð, m.ep-stem, [HELETH]; man, hero, 56, 177 etc (nom.pl.)

hǣste*, adv., violently 263n.

hǣðen, adj., HEATHEN 98, 110, 179, 216.

hē, pron.m. HE 4 etc; hēo, pron.f., 2 etc. his (gen.sg.) 16 etc; hyre (gen.sg.) 127, 172. him (dat.sg.) 53, 60 etc; hyre (dat.sg.) 5, 97 etc. hyne (acc.sg.) 13, 44 etc; hīe (acc.sg.) 4, 170; hit (acc. sg.n.) 130; hyt 174. hī (acc.sg.) 94, 150.

hēafod, n.a-stem, HEAD 110, 126, 173, 179.

hēafodgerīm, n.a-stem, [+ RIME]; number of heads, greatest number, 308.

hēafodweard, m.a-stem, chief guardian 239.

hēah, adj., HIGH 43 (dat.sg.), 161 (acc.sg.); hēhsta (sup.) 4, 94; hȳhsta 308.

healdan, hēoldon (pret.) 142; v.(7), HOLD, keep.

healdend, m.nd-stem, leader 289.

healf, adj., HALF 105.

hēan, adj., humble, poor. 234 n.

hēap, m.a-stem, HEAP; crowd 163.

heard, adj., HARD 79; sharp 263; brave 225. hearde, adv., grievously 116, 216.

hearra, m.n-stem, [HER]; lord 56.

heaðorinc, m.a-stem, warrior. 179, 212.

hēawan, hēowon (pret.) 303, v.(7), HEW, slay. gehēawan, v.(7), slay 90, 289, 294 (p.part.).

hellebryne, m.i-stem, HELL + [BRUNE]; hellfire 116.

helm, m.a-stem, HELM, helmet, 193, 203 etc.

help, f.ō-stem, HELP 96.

heofon, m.a-stem, HEAVEN 343.

heolfrig, adj., gory 130, 316.

heolstor, adj., dark 121.

heorte, f.n-stem, HEART 87.

heoruwǣpen, n.a-stem, WEAPON, sword, 263.

hēr, adv., HERE 177, 285, 289.

hērbūend, m.nd-stem, dweller on earth 96.

here, m.ja-stem, [HERE]; army 135, 161, 293.

herefolc, *n.a-stem,* army 234, 239.

hereréaf, *n.a-stem,* [HERE *sb.* + REIF]; plunder, booty, 316.

herewǽða, *m.n-stem,* warrior 126, 173.

herpað, *m.a-stem,* [+ PATH]; war-path, passage for the army, 302.

heteþoncol, *adj.,* [HATE *sb.*[1] +]; hostile 105.

hīe, *pron.nom.pl.,* they 10 *etc;* **heora** *(gen.pl.)* 38, 56; **hyra** 128 *etc;* **hira** 274; **him** *(dat.pl.)* 38 *etc.*

hige, *m.i-stem,* [HIGH *sb.*[1]]; mind, heart, 87.

higeróf, *adj.,* valiant 302.

higeþoncol, *adj.,* wise, thoughtful, 131.

hild, *f.jō-stem,* battle 251, 293.

hildeléoð, *n.a-stem,* [+ LEOTH]; battle-song 211.

hildenǽdre, *f.n-stem,* [+*ADDER*]; battle-adder, arrow, 222.

hinsīð, *m.a-stem,* [+ SITHE]; departure, death, 117n.

hlāford, *m.a-stem,* LORD 251.

hlanc, *adj.,* LANK, lean, 205.

hlǽstan, *w.v.(1),* [cf LAST, *v.*]; adorn 36.

hlihhan, hlóh *(pret.)* 23; *v.(6),* [cf LAUGH]; laugh, rejoice triumphantly.

hlimman, *v.(3),* resound 205.

hlūde, *adv.,* LOUD, loudly, 205, 223, 270.

hlȳdan, hlȳdde *(pret.)* 23; *w.v.* *(1),* [cf LIDE]; clamour.

hlynnan, *w.v.(1),* [cf LINN[1]]; shout, roar, 23.

hogian, *w.v.(2),* have in mind 250, 273.

hopian, *w.v.(2),* HOPE 117.

hornboga, *m.n-stem,* [HORN+ BOW]; bow tipped with horn *or* curved like a horn 222.

hosp, *m.a-stem,* insult, contumely, 216.

hraðe, *adv.,* [RATHE, cf RATHER]; quickly 37.

hrægl, *n.a-stem,* [RAIL]; armour 282.

hrǽw, *m.n.wa-stem,* corpse 313.

hrefn, *m.a-stem,* RAVEN 206.

hrēodan, gehroden *(p.part.)* 37; *v.(2),* adorn.

hrēoh, *adj.,* [REH]; furious 282.

hrēowigmód, *adj.,* sad, sorrowful, 289.

hreðer, *n.* ?, breast 94.

hring, *m.a-stem,* RING 37.

hróf, *m.a-stem,* ROOF 67.

hū, *adv.,* HOW 25, 75 *etc.*

hund, *m.a-stem,* HOUND; dog 110

hupseax, *n.a-stem,* cf HIP; hipsword, short sword, 327.

hūru, *adv.,* certainly 345.

hwā, hwǽne *(acc.sg.)* 52; *pron.,* WHO; some one. **gehwǽne,** each one *(acc.sg.)* 186.

gehwā, gehwǽne *(acc.sg.)* 186, *pron.,* each one.

hwealf, *adj.,* hollow 214.

hwearf, *m.a-stem,* [WHARF *sb.*[2]]; crowd 249.

hweorfan, hwearf *(pret.)* 112n· *v.(2),* [WHARVE]; depart.

hwīl, *f.ō-stem,* WHILE, time, 214.

gehwylc, *pron.,* each, all, 32. *ānra gehwylcne,* each one 95.

hyht, *m.a-stem,* [HIGHT *sb.*[3]]; hope 98.

hyhtwynn, *f.i-* or *jō-stem,* joy of hope, joy, 121.

hyldo *f.īn-stem,* favour, grace, *(gen.sg.).*

gehȳran, *w.v.(1),* HEAR 24, 160

hyrde, *m.ja-stem,* HERD; guardian 60.

hyrnednebba, *m.n-stem,* hornbeaked one 212.

hyrst, *f.i-stem,* war-equipment. 316.

GLOSSARY

I

ic, *pron.,* 17, 83 *etc;* **mē** *(dat.sg.)* 85, 86 *etc.*

ides, *f.ō-(orig.i-)stem,* woman 14, 109 *etc.*

in, *prep.w.dat. or instr.,* IN 2, 116 *etc; w.acc.* 193, 225, 276. **in,** *adv.,* 150, 170.

inn, *n.a-stem,* INN; chamber 70.

inne, *adv.,* in 45, 50.

inwidd, *adj.,* wicked 28.

irnan, urnon *(pret.pl.)* 164; *v.(3),* [ERN]; run.

Iudith, *prop.name,* Judith 13, 123 *etc.*

L

landbūend, *m.nd-stem,* inhabitant, native, 226, 314.

lang, *adj.,* LONG; **lengra** *(comp.)* 184. **lange,** *adv.,* long 158, 346. **lēng** *(comp.)* 153.

lār, *f.ō-stem,* LORE¹, counsel 333.

lāst, *m.a-stem,* [LAST sb.¹]; footprint, track, 297. *on lāst,* behind, after, 209, 291.

late, *adv.,* LATE 275.

lāð, *adj.,* LOATH, hateful, hostile, 45, 72 *etc.* **lāðost** *(sup.)* 322; **lāðestan**(*gen.sg.*)178; (*dat.pl.*) 314.

lǣdan, *w.v.(1),* LEAD, bring, 42, 72 *etc.*

lǣtan, *v.(7),* LET 221 *(pret.pl.).*

lǣðð, *f.jā-stem,* [LETH]; affliction, wrong, 158, 184.

gelēafa, *m.n-stem,* [LEVE]; belief, faith, 6, 89 *etc.*

lēan, *n.a-stem,* [LEAN sb.¹]; reward 346.

lēap, *m.a-stem,* [LEAP sb.²]; trunk, body, 111.

lēas, *adj.w.gen.,* [LEESE]; bereft of, without, 121.

lēode, *m.i-stem.(pl.),* [LEDE]; people 147, 178.

lēodhata, *m.n-stem,* [LEDE +]; tyrant 72.

lēof, *adj.,* [LIEF]; dear 147, 346.

lēoht, *adj.,* LIGHT, bright, radiant, 191.

lēoma, *m.n-stem,* [LEAM]; beam of light 191.

libban, lyfdon *(pret.pl.)* 296; *w.v.(3),* LIVE.

licgan, lāgon *(pret.pl.)* 30; *v.(5),* LIE 278 *etc;* **læg** *(pret.sg.)* 106, 111, 293; **līð** *(3p.sg.pres.)* 288.

līf, *n.a-stem,* LIFE 184, 280 *etc.*

lind, *f.ō-stem,* [LIND]; shield 191, 303 *etc.*

lindwiggend, *m.nd-stem,* warrior 42, 297.

list, *f.i-stem,* LIST sb.² ; **listum** *(dat.pl. used adv.),* cunningly, skilfully, 101.

gelōme, *adv.,* [Y-LOME]; repeatedly 18.

losian, *w.v.(2),* [LOSE v.¹]; perish 287.

lungre, *adv.,* soon, forthwith, 147, 280.

lust, *m.a-stem*(orig.u-stem), LUST, desire, joy, 161n.

lyft, *f.i-stem or m.a-stem,* [LIFT sb.¹]; air 347.

gelystan, *w.v.(1) (impersonal w. acc. of pers. + gen. of thing),* LIST v.¹ ; desire. *gelyste (pret. sg.)* 306.

lȳthwōn, *n.w.gen.,* few 310.

M

magan, mæg *(1sg.pres.)* 152; **magon** *(2pl.)* 177; **mihte** *(3sg.pret.)* 102; **mihton** *(pl.)* 235; **mæge** *(subj.pres.)* 330; **mihte** *(subj.pret.)* 49, 75; **mihten** *(subj.pret.pl.)* 24, 136; *pret.pres.(5),* MAY, can.

magoþegn, *m.a-stem,* [THANE]; retainer 236.

man, *m.monos-stem*, MAN[1] 52, 181 *etc.*

manian, *w.v.(2)*, admonish, exhort, 26.

manna, *m.n-stem*, man 98, 101.

māðm (mādum), *m.a-stem*, [MADME]; treasure, jewel, 318, 329, 340.

mægen, *n.a-stem*, MAIN *sb.*[1]; armed force 253, 261.

mægenēacen, *adj.*, mighty, vigorous, 292.

mægð, *f.et-stem*, maiden 35, 43 *etc., gen.s.* 333.

mægð, *f.ō-stem*, [MAYTH]; tribe 324.

mære, *adj.*, sublime, illustrious, 3; **mærra** (*comp.*) 329; **mærost** (*sup.*) 324.

mærð, *f.ō-stem*, glory 343.

mæst, see **micel**.

mēce, *m.ja-stem*, sword 78, 104.

mēd, *f.ō-stem*, MEED, reward, 334, 343.

medoburg, *f.i-stem*, MEAD + BOROUGH; mead-city, rejoicing city, 167.

medowērig, *adj.*, MEAD + WEARY; drunken with mead 229; 245.

medugāl, *adj.*, MEAD [+ GOLE]; mead-excited, drunk, 26.

mēowle, *f.n-stem*, maiden, woman, 56, 261.

metod, *m.a-stem*, Creator, God, 154, 261.

micel, *adj.*, MICKLE, much, great, 10, 70 *etc*; *māra* (*comp.*) 92; *mæst* (*sup.*) 3, 181 *etc*; **mā* (*adv.comp.*) 329*.

mid, *prep.w.dat. or instr.*, [MID]; 29, 59 *etc.*

middan, see **onmiddan**.

mihtig, *adj.*, MIGHTY 92, 198.

milts, *f.jō-stem*, [MILCE]; grace, mercy, 85, 92, 349.

mīn, *adj.*, MINE; my 90, 94, 198.

mōd, *n.a-stem*, MOOD *sb.*[1]; heart 57, 93 *etc.*

mōdig, *adj.*, [MOODY]; daring, proud, 26, 52, 334.

molde, *f.n-stem*, MOULD *sb.*[1]; earth 343.

mon, *m.*, see **man**.

mon, *indef.pron.*, [MAN, *indef. pron.*; cf ONE 21]; one, they, 291.

mōnað, *m.-þ-stem*, MONTH 324.

gemong, *n.a-stem*, troop 193, 303. *gemang* 225.

morgencolla, *m.n-stem*, morning terror 245.

morgentīd, *f.i-stem*, MORN + TIDE; morning 236.

morðor, *n.a-stem*, MURDER; torment, sin, 90, 181.

mōt, *pret.pres.(6)*, [MOTE[1]]; may, must, 89 (*subj.*); 118 (*subj.*); **mōste** (*pret.*) 185.

mund, *f.ō-stem*, [MUND]; hand 229.

mundbyrd, *f.i-stem*, protection 3.

murnan, *v.(3)*, MOURN 154.

gemyndig, *adj.*, [MINDY]; mindful 74.

myntan, *w.v.(1)*, [MINT]; think, suppose, 253.

N

nāhte, see **āgan**.

nama, *m.n-stem*, NAME 81.

nān, *pron.*, NONE 68, 233, 257.

næfre, *adv.*, NEVER 91.

nænig, *pron.*, no one 51.

næs, see **wesan**.

næs, *m.a-stem*, NESS; cliff, headland, 113.

ne, *adv.*, [NE]; not 20, 59 *etc.*

ne, *conj.*, [NE]; nor 234.

nēah, *adj.*, NIGH; near 287 (*used*

48

GLOSSARY

as adv.); **nēar** *(comp.)* 53;
nēhsta *(sup.)*, last 73.
ġeneahhe, *adv.*, frequently 26.
nēalǣcan, *w.v.(1)*, [NEHLECHE];
approach 34, 261.
nēhsta, see **nēah.**
nemnan, *w.v.(1)*, [NEMN]; name,
call, 81.
nēosan, *w.v.(1)*, visit 63 *(w.gen.).*
neowol, *adj.*, [NUEL]; deep, abys-
mal, 113.
nerġend, *m.nd-stem*, Saviour, 45,
73, 81.
nest, *n.* (ON *nest*), provisions,
food.
nēðan, *w.v.(1)*, venture, dare,
risk, 277.
niht, *f.monos-stem*, NIGHT 34, 64.
nihtes *(used adv.)*, at night 45.
niman, *v.(4)*, [NIM]; capture 313.
ġeniman, *v.(4)*, capture 77, 98.
nīð, *m.a-stem*, [NITH]; strife, war,
53; evil, iniquity, 34 *(instr.*
gen.); affliction, trouble, 287.
nīðheard, *adj.*, bold, daring,
277.
nīðhycġend, *m.nd-stem*, evil-
schemer 233.
nīwian, *w.v.(2)*, [NEW *v.*]; renew
98.
nō, *adv.*, NO, not at all, 117.
nū, *adv.*, NOW 92, 186, 287.
nū ðā, now 86.
nȳd, *f.i-stem*, NEED 277.
nymðe, *conj.*, unless 52.
nyste, see **witan.**
nyðerian, *w.v.(2)*, NITHER,
abase, bring low, oppress, 113.

O

of, *prep.w.dat.*, OF 70, 135; from
79, 119, 149, 203, 222, 230,
335.
ofdūne, *adv.*, down 290.
ofer, *prep.w.acc.*, OVER 161; *ofer*

ealne dæg, throughout the day
28.
ofercuman, *v.(4)*, OVERCOME
235.
oferdrencan, *w.v.(1)*,+DRENCH;
intoxicate, inebriate, 31.
oferwinnan, oferwunnen *(p.*
part.) 319; *v.(3)*, [OVERWIN];
conquer.
ofost, *f.ō-stem*, haste 10, 70.
ofstum, in haste 35 *(used*
adv.).
ofstlīce, *adv.*, forthwith 150,
169.
on, *prep.¹w.dat.*, ON, in 5, 13 *etc*;
into 57; from 314; on 65, 294,
297, 319; upon 209. *²w.acc.*, on
50, 51, 111, 145, 178, 307, 312;
to 54, 300; in 130, 291; at 204,
236, 306.
on, *adv.*, in 129.
on . . . middan, *prep.w.dat.*,
AMID, upon, 68.
onbryrdan, *w.v.(1)*, inspire, in-
vite, 95.
ōnettan, *w.v.(1)*, hasten 162; 139
(3pl.pret.).
onġēan, *prep.w.acc.*, AGAIN B 3;
towards 165.
onġinnan, *v.(3)*, [ONGIN]; begin
42, 80 *etc.*
onġitan, onġēaton *(pret.)* 168,
238; *v.(5)*, [ANGET]; learn, per-
ceive.
onhǣtan, *w.v.(1)*, [+ HEAT]; in-
flame 87.
oninnan, *prep.w.acc.*, among
312.
onlēon, onlēah *(pret.)* 124;
v.(1), grant.
onufan, *adv.*, [ANOVEN]; above
252.
onwæcnan, onwōce *(pret.subj.)*
77; *v.(6)*, [AWAKEN]; awake.
onwrīðan, *v.(1)*, unwrap, dis-
close, 173.

49

orc, *m.a-stem*, pitcher, cup 18.

ōretmæcg, *m.a-stem*, warrior 232.

orfeorme, *adj.w.instr.*, destitute of, lacking, 271.

orsāwle, *adj.*, [+ SOUL]; lifeless, dead, 108.

oð, *conj.* used in oðþæt, until 30, 33, 134, 238. oð, *conj.*, until 140, 292.

ōþer, *adj.*, OTHER 109.

oððe, *conj.*, or 259, 339.

oðþringan, oðþrong (*pret.*) 185; *v.(3)*, *w.dat. of pers. and acc. of thing*, deprive of.

R

randwiggend, *m.nd-stem*, warrior, 11, 20, 188.

rǣd, *m.a-stem*, [REDE]; sense 68 (*gen.pl.*); good advice, wisdom, reason, 97.

ræfnan, *w.v.(1)*, perform 11.

rǣswa, *m.n-stem*, leader, chief, 12, 178.

rēad, *adj.*, RED 338.

recene, *adv.*, immediately 188.

gerēnian, *w.v.(2)*, adorn 338.

rēocan, *v.(2)*, REEK 313 (*pres. part.*).

rest, *f.jō-stem*, REST, bed, couch, 54, 68.

restan, *w.v.(1)*, REST 44, 321.

rēðe, *adj.*, [RETHE]; terrible, raging, 348.

rīce, *adj.*, [RICH]; powerful, mighty, 11, 20 *etc.*

rīce, *n.ja-stem*, [RICHE]; kingdom 343.

riht, *adj.*, RIGHT, true, 97.

geriht, *n.a-stem*, straight direction; *on gerihte*, straight away 202.

rinc, *m.a-stem*, [RINK]; warrior, man, 54, 338.

rodor, *m.a-stem*, heaven 5, 348.

rōf, *adj.*, strong, brave, 20, 53.

rondwiggend, see randwiggend.

rūm, *adj.*, [ROOM *a.*]; spacious, wide, 348.

rūm, *m.a-stem*, ROOM (*sb.*), opportunity, scope, 313.

rūme, *adv.*, spaciously, wide and light; *wearð hyre rūme on mōde*, she felt a great relief, 97.

rūn, *f.ō-stem*, [ROUN]; council 54.

S

sacu, sæcce (*f.dat.*) 288; *f.ō-stem*, [SAKE[4]]; strife, battle.

salowigpād, *adj.*, with dark feathers 211.

sār, *adj.*, SORE, grievous, 183.

sǣgan, *w.v.(1)*, fell, destroy, 293.

sǣlan, *w.v.(1)*, [SEAL *v.*[2]]; bind, fetter, 114.

sceacan, *v.(6)*, [SHAKE]; hasten 291.

sceal 119; sculon (*pres.pl.*) 287; sceolde (*pret.sg.*) 63; *pret. pres.(4)*, SHALL, SHOULD; was to 63; have to 119, 287.

scealc, *m.a-stem*, [SHALK], man, retainer, 230.

scearp, *adj.*, SHARP 78.

scēað, *f.ō-stem*, SHEATH 79, 230.

sceaða, *m.n-stem*, [SCATHE]; enemy 193.

scēotend, *m.nd-stem*, [cf SHOOT *v.*]; shooter, warrior, 304.

sceran, scæron (*pret.pl.*) 304; *v.(4)*, [SHEAR], cut, cleave.

gescieppan, gesceōþ (*pret.*) 347; *v.(6)*, [I-SHAPE]; create.

scild, *m.u-stem*, SHIELD 204.

scildburh, *f.i-stem*, phalanx, shield-wall, 304.

scīr, *adj.*, [SHIRE *a.*]; bright, gleaming, 193.

scīrmǣled, *adj.*, brightly adorned 230.

scūr, *m.a-stem*, SHOWER, storm of battle, 79n., 221.

scȳne, *adj.*, [SHEEN]; beautiful 316.

scyppend, *m.nd-stem*, Creator 78.

sě, *def.art.m.*, the 9, 20, 25, 28 *etc.* sěo, *f.nom.sg.* þæt, *neut.sg.* þæs, *m.g.sg.*, 4, 47 *etc.* þām, *m.d.sg.*, 3, 7 *etc.* þone, *acc.sg* þǣre, *f.gen.sg.* þǣre, *f.d.sg.* þā, *f.acc.sg.* þæs, *neut.gen.sg.*, 5, 20, 239; 341, 346 (*for that*). þām, *neut.d.sg.* þæt, *neut.acc. sg.* þȳ, *m.instr.*   . þě, *neut. instr.* þon 92. þā, *nom.pl.* þāra, *gen.pl.* þām, *dat.pl.* þā, *acc.pl.*, 10.

sě, *rel.pron.m.*, that. þæt, *neut. acc.sg.*, 331, 338. sěþe, *rel. pron.* þāþe 238, 296 *etc.*

searoðoncol, *adj.*, shrewd, wise 145, 330.

sěcan, *w.v.*(*1*), SEEK 96.

gesěcan, gesōhte (*pret.*) 14; *w.v.*(*1*), [ISECHE]; visit.

secg, *m.ja-stem*, [SEGGE]; man 201.

secgan, sægde (*pret.*) 341; *w.v.*(*3*), SAY, tell, ascribe, 152.

sendan, *w.v.*(*1*), SEND 190, 224.

gesěon, *v.*(*5*), SEE 136.

sīd, *adj.*, [SIDE *a.*]; ample, wide, 337.

sigefolc, *n.a-stem*, victorious people 152.

sigerōf, *adj.*, victorious 177.

sigeþūf*, *m.a-stem*, triumphant banner 201.*

sigewong, *m.a-stem*, field of victory 294.

sigor, *m.a-stem*, victory 89, 124, 298.

sigorlěan, *n.a-stem*, reward of victory 344.

sīn, *pron.adj.*, his, her, 29, 99, 132.

sinc, *n.a-stem*, treasure 30, 339.

singan, sang (*pret.*) 211; *v.*(*3*), SING.

sittan, sǣton (*pret.*) 141; sǣte (*subj.pret.*) 252; *v.*(*5*), SIT 15; settled down on 252.

sīð, *m.a-stem*, [SITHE]; journey 145; time 73, 109.

sīð, *adv.*, late, tardily, 275.

gesīð, *m.a-stem*, companion, retainer, 201.

sīðfæt, *m.n.a-stem*, [SITHE + VAT]; journey, expedition, 335.

slǣp, *m.a-stem*, SLEEP 247.

slěan, slōh (*pret.sg.*) 103, 108; slōgon (*pret.pl.*) 231; *v.*(*6*), SLAY, strike.

geslěan, geslegene (*p.part.*) 31; *v.*(*6*), strike down, smite.

slegefǣge, *adj.*, [SLAY + FEY]; doomed to perish 247.

snell, *adj.*, [SNELL]; keen, active, 199.

snotor, *adj.*, [SNOTER]; prudent 55, 125.

snūde, *adv.*, quickly, at once, 55, 125, 199.

somod, *adv.*, [SAMED]; together 163, 269 *etc.*

sorg, *f.ō-stem*, SORROW, distress, 88, 182.

sōð, *adj.*, SOOTH, true, 89, 344.

sparian, *w.v.*(*2*), SPARE 233.

spōwan, spěow (*pret.*) 274; *v.*(*7*), *impers.*, avail, help.

sprecan, *v.*(*5*), SPEAK, 160, 176.

standan, stōdon (*pret.*) 267; *v.*(*6*), STAND.

starian, *w.v.*(*2*), STARE, gaze, 179*.

stěap, *adj.*, STEEP; deep 17.

stedeheard, *adj.*, firm, strong, 223.

steppan, stŏpon (*pret.pl.*) 39, 69 *etc*; *v.*(6), STEP, march.

stercedferhŏ, *adj.*, determined, resolute, 55, 227.

stiŏmŏd, *adj.*, [STITH *a.* + MOOD]; stern, fierce, 25.

strǣl, *m.a-stem*, [STREAL]; arrow 223.

strēam, *m.a-stem*, STREAM; sea (*pl.*) 348.

gestẏran, *w.v.*(*1*), *w.dat. of pers. and gen. of thing*, restrain, prevent, 60.

styrman, *w.v.*(*1*), STURME; storm, rage, 25, 223.

styrnmŏd, *adj.*, STERN of MOOD 227.

sum, *pron.*, SOMEone, a certain, 148, 275.

sundoryrfe, *m.ja-stem*, [cf SUNDER + ERF[1]]; private inheritance 339.

sŭsl, *n.a-stem*, torment, torture, 114.

swă, *conj.*, SO, as, that, 38, 95 *etc.*

swă, *adv.*, SO 67, 126, 130.

swătig, *adj.*, [SWOTY]; gory 337.

swaŏu, *f.ŏ-stem*, [SWATH[1]]; track, path-way, 321.

swǣsendo, *neut.pl.*, banquet 9.

swegel, *n.a-stem*, heaven 80, 88 *etc.*

swēora, *m.n-stem*, neck 106.

sweorcendferhŏ, *adj.*, sombre, sad, 269.

sweord, *n.a-stem*, SWORD, 89, 288 *etc*; **swyrd** 230, 317 *etc.*

swēot, *n.a-stem*, troop, army, 298.

sweotole, *adv.*, [cf SUTEL]; clearly 177.

sweotollice, *adv.*, [cf SUTE-LICHE]; clearly 136.

swĭma, *m.n-stem*, [SWIME]; SWOON 30, 106.

swĭŏ, *adj.*, [SWITH]; strong. **swĭŏre**, (*comp.*), right 80.

swĭŏlĭc, *adj.*, violent 240.

swĭŏmŏd, *adj.*, arrogant, insolent, 30, 339.

swiŏrian, geswiŏrod (*p.part.*) 266; *w.v.*(*2*), [cf SWITHER *v.*[1]]; diminish, destroy.

swutelian, *w.v.*(*2*), [SUTELE]; reveal, manifest, 285.

swylc, *pron.*, SUCH, such as, 65.

swylce, *conj.*, [SUCH]; as 18, as if 31.

swyrd, see **sweord**.

swyrdgeswing, *n.a-stem*, [+ SWING *sb.*]; sword-brandishing 240.

swẏŏe, *adv.*, [SWITH]; greatly 88; **swẏŏor** (*comp.*) 182.

sẏ, syndon, see **bēon**.

sylf, *pron.*, SELF 204, 285, 335, 349.

symbel, symle (*dat.sg.*) 15; *n.a-stem*; feast, banquet.

symbel, *adj.*, *used as neut.noun*, continuous. *on symbel*, always 44.

gesynto, *f.jŏ-stem*, salvation 90 (*gen.pl.*).

syŏŏan, *conj.*, [SITHEN]; as soon as 160, 168 *etc.*

syŏŏan, *adv.*, SITHEN; after 114.

T

tăcnian, *w.v.*(*2*), [TOKEN]; betoken, signify, 197, 286.

tēon, tēah (*pret.*) 99; *v.*(*2*), [TEE *v.*[1]]; draw, pull.

teran, *v.*(*4*), TEAR 281.

tĭd, *f.i-stem*, TIDE; time 286, 306.

tilian, *w.v.*(*2*), [TILL], provide 208.

tĭr, *m.a-stem*, glory 93, 157, 197, 272.

tīð, *f.ō-stem*, TITHE *sb.*[2]; boon, grant, 6. *tīðe gefremede*, granted.

tō, *prep.w.dat.*, TO 9, 11, 15, 16 *etc*; in 7, 322, 345; as 96, 174, 295, 296, 334; for 120, 200, 248. *before inf. tō berenne* 131, 313. tō ðām, so, to such an extent, 275.

tōbrēdan, *v.(3)*, [TOBRAID]; cast off 247n. (*inf.*).

tōgēanes, *prep.w.dat.*, [TOGAINS]; toward 149.

tohte, *f.n-stem*, conflict, battle, 197.

torht, *adj.*, [TORHT]; illustrious 43.

torhtlīc, *adj.*, splendid 157.

torhtmōd, *adj.*, [TORHT +]; glorious 6, 93.

torn, *n.a-stem*, grief, rage, 272.

torne, *adv.*, bitterly, grievously, 93.

tōð, *m.monos.-stem*, TOOTH 272 (*dat.pl.*).

tōweard, *adj.*, [TOWARD *a.*]; approaching 157, 286.

træf, *n.a-stem*, tent, pavilion, 43, 255, 268.

trum, *adj.*, firm 6.

twēogan, twēode (*pret.*) 1, 345; *w.v.(2)*, doubt.

þ

þā, *adv.*, [THO]; then 2, 7, 15 *etc*.

þā, *conj.*, [THO, *adv.(conj.)*]; when 3, 145.

geþafian, *w.v.(2)* [I-THAVE]; allow, consent to, 60.

þancolmōd, *adj.*, attentive 172.

þanonne, *adv.*, [THENNE]; thence, away, 132.

þāþe, *rel. pron.*, see sē, *rel.pron.*

þǣr, *adv.*, THERE 2, 17, 46, 113, 119, 284, 307.

þǣr, *conj.*, where 40, 44, 63.

þæs þe, *conj.*, since, from the time that, 13, because 344.

þæt, *conj.*, THAT 4, 48 *etc* (always þ').

þe, *rel.pron.*, [THE *part.3*]; who, which, that, 50, 71, 96 *etc*.

þe, *conj.*, because 6, that 287.

þe, *part.*, see sē, *rel.pron.* and þæs þe. Used pleonastically in þe nēar 53.

þēah, *adv.*, [cf THOUGH B.1]; however, nevertheless, 257.

þēah, *conj.*, [cf THOUGH,]; though 20.

þearf, *f.ō-stem*, [THARF]; need 3, 92.

þearf, þyrfen (*subj.pres.pl.*) 153; *pret.pres.(3)*, [THARF]; need 117.

þearfende, *adj.*, needy 85* (*f.dat.sg.*).

þearle, *adj.*, very 74, 86, 262, 268, 306.

þearlmōd, *adj.*, severe, mighty 66, 91.

þēaw, *m.wa-stem*, [THEW[1]]; virtue 129.

þegn, *m.a-stem*, THANE, retainer 10, 306.

þencan, þōhte (*pret.sg.*) 58; þōhton (*pret.pl.*) 208; *w.v.(1)*, THINK, intend.

þenden, *conj.*, while 66.

þēoden, *m.a-stem*, LORD 3; King 66, 91 *etc*.

þēodguma, *m.n-stem*, [THEDE + GOME]; man, warrior, 208, 331.

þēowen, *f.ō-stem*, [cf THEOW]; handmaiden 74.

þes, *dem.adj.*, THIS; ðysse, *f.dat. sg.*, 66. þysne, *m.acc.sg.*, 90. ðys, *m.instr.sg.*, 2, 89. þyssa, *gen.pl.*, 187.

þicgan, þēgon (*pret.*) 19; *v.(5)*, receive.

þīn, *poss.pron.*, THINE, thy, 85, 91.

þīnen, *f.ō-stem*, handmaiden 172.

þing, *n.a-stem*, THING, deed, event, 60, 153.

þolian, *w.v.(2)*, [THOLE]; suffer, endure, 215 (*pret.*); 272 (*pres. part.*).

þon, see sē, *def.art.*

þonan, *adv.*, thence 118; cf þanonne.

geþonc, *m.a-stem*, [I-THANK]; thought, mind, 13.

þoncwyrðe, *adj.*, THANK-WORTHY, deserving of gratitude, 153.

þonne, *conj.*, THAN 329.

þrāg, *f.ō-stem*, [THROW *sb.*¹]; time; *ealle þrage*, continuously 237.

þrēat, *m.a-stem*, [THREAT *sb.*]; troop 62, 164.

þringan, þrungon (*pret.*) 164; *v.(3)*, [THRING]; throng, press forward, 249; geþrungen (*p. part.*) 287.

þrym, *m.a-stem*, [THRUM *sb.*¹]; glory, majesty, 60, 86; power 331; troop 164.

þrymful, *adj.*, majestic, glorious, 74.

þrymlic, *adj.*, magnificent 8.

þrȳnes, *f.jō-stem*, [THREENESS, THRINNESS]; Trinity 86.

þū, *pron.*, THOU; þē (*acc.sg.*) 83.

geþungen, *p.part.* (of þēon), accomplished, excellent, 129.

þurh, *prep.w.acc.*, THROUGH 151, 303; 49 (*adv.* ?); by means of 186, 198, 333, 349.

þus, *adv.*, THUS 93.

þūsendmǣlum, *adv.*, [THOU-SAND + -MEAL, *suffix*]; by thousands 165.

þyder, *adv.*, THITHER 129.

þystre, *adj.*, [THESTER]; dark, gloomy, 34.

þystru, *f-īn-stem*, [THESTER *sb*]; darkness 118.

U

under, *prep.w.dat.*, UNDER 67, 203, 219, 332; *w.acc.* 113.

unlǣd, *adj.*, miserable 102.

unlyfigende, *adj.*, lifeless, dead, 180, 315.

unnan, ūðe (*pret.*) 123, 183; *pret. pres.(3)*, [UNNE]; grant.

geunnan, *pret.pres.(3)*, [UNNE]; grant, 90 (*imper.*).

unrōt, *adj.*, dejected 284.

unsōfte, *adv.*, [UN¹ııb + SOFT]; harshly, cruelly, 228.

unswǣslīc, *adj.*, ungentle, cruel, 65.

unsȳfre, *adj.*, unclean, impure, 76.

ūp, *adv.*, UP 9.

ūre, see wē.

ūrigfeðere, *adj.*, dewy-winged 210.

urnon, see irnan.

ūs, see we.

ūt of, *prep.w.dat.*, OUT OF 70, 135.

ūte, *adv.*, outside 284.

W

wald, *m.u-stem*, WOLD, forest, 206.

waldend, *m.nd-stem*, [WALD-END], Lord 5, 61.

wann, *adj.*, [WAN], dark 206.

wæccan, wæccende (*pres.part.*) 142; *w.v.(1)*, WATCH.

wælgīfre, *adj.*, [WAL +]; greedy for slaughter 207, 295.

wælscel, (?), carnage 312.

wǣpen, *n.a-stem*, WEAPON 290.

wǣrloga, *m.n-stem*, [WARLOCK]; troth-breaker, traitor, 71.

54

GLOSSARY

wĕ, *pron.*, WE 287; ūre (*gen.pl.*)
285, 289; ūs (*dat.pl.*) 181,
184.

wĕagesĭŏ, *m.a-stem*, [cf WOE +];
companion in misery 16.

gewealdan, *v.(7)*, *w.gen.*, [cf
WIELD]; control, manage, 103.

wealgeat, *n.a-stem*, [WALL +
GATE]; rampart-gate 141.

weall, *m.a-stem*, WALL (*sb.¹*) 137,
151, 161.

weard, *m.a-stem*, [WARD]; guar-
dian 80.

weard, *f.ō-stem*, WARD (*sb.²*),
watch, 142.,

weard, *adv.*, see wiŏ.

wegan, wǣgon (*pret.*) 325;
v.(5), [WEIGH *v.¹*]; carry.

wel, *adv.*, WELL 27, 103.

wēnan, *w.v.(1)*, *w.gen.*, WEEN;
expect, apprehend, 20.

weorpan, wurpon (*pret.*) 290;
v.(3), [WARP]; cast, fling.

weorŏan, wearþ (*pret.*) 21, 57
etc. wurdon (*pret.pl.*) 159;
geworden (*p.part*) 260n; *v.(3)*,
[WORTH]; become, be, fare,
(260n.).

weorŏian, geweorŏod (*p.part.*)
298; *w.v.(2)*, [I-WURTHI];
honour.

weorŏmynd, *f.ō-stem*, [WORTH-
MINT]; honour 342.

wer, *m.a-stem*, [WERE *sb.¹*]; man
71, 142 etc.

wērigferhŏ, *adj.*, [WEARY +];
weary, cast down, 249*, 290.

werod, *n.a-stem*, [WERED]; troop,
host, 199, 342.

wesan, wæs (*pret.sg.*) 12, 46 etc;
with neg. næs 107, 257; wǣron
(*pret.pl.*) 17, 225 etc; wǣron
(*subj.pret.pl.*) 31; to be.

wīd, *adj.*, WIDE, enduring; tō
wīdan aldre, for ever and ever
347.

wīde, *adv.*, WIDE, far and wide,
156.

wīdl, *m. or n.a-stem*, defilement
59.

wīf, *n.a-stem*, WIFE; woman 148,
163.

wiga, *m.n-stem*, warrior, man, 49.

wiggend, *m.nd-stem*, warrior 69,
141 etc.

wiht, *adv.*, [WIGHT], ne wiht, not
at all 274.

willa, *m.n-stem*, WILL (*sb.¹*),
pleasure 295.

wīn, *n-a-stem*, WINE 29, 67.

wind, *m.a-stem*, WIND 347.

windan, wand (*pret.*) 110; *v.(3)*,
WIND; roll.

winedryhten, *m.a-stem*, lord
and friend 274.

wīngedrinc, *n.a-stem*, wine-
drinking 16.

wīnhāte, *f.n-stem*, invitation to
wine 8.

wīnsæd, *adj.*, [WINE + SAD];
satiated with wine 71.

witan, wistan (*pret.*) 207*; *pret.
pres.(1)*, [WIT]; know; with neg.
nyste 68.

gewītan, *v.(1)*, [I-WITE *vb.²*];
depart 61, 145. gewitan
(*3pl. pret.*) 290.

wīte, *n.ja-stem*, [WITE *sb.²*]; tor-
ment 115.

gewitloca, *m.n-stem*, mind 69.

wiŏ, *prep.w.acc.*, WITH 260;
w.gen., against, toward, 4, 99,
162, 248. wiŏ . . . weard, to-
ward 99.

wiŏertrod, *n.a-stem*, [WITHER-¹,
prefix, + TROD *sb.*]; retreat
312.

wlanc, *adj.*, [WLONK]; stately,
proud, 16, 325.

wlītan, *v.(1)*, look 49.

wlitig, *adj.*, [cf WLITE]; beautiful
137, 255.

wolcen, *m.n.a-stem,* WELKIN; cloud 67.

wolde, *pret.,* WOULD 59, 183; **wylle** (*1sg.pres.*) 84, 187.

wom, *m.n.a-stem,* [WAM]; sin 59.

womfull, *adj.,* foul 77.

word, *n.a-stem,* WORD 82, 151 *etc.*

worn, *m.a-stem,* multitude 163.

woruld, *f.ō-stem,* WORLD 66, 156.

woruldbūend, *m.nd-stem,* world-dweller 82.

gewrecan, *v.(5),* WREAK, avenge, 92.

wreccan, wrehton (*pret.pl.*) 228, 243; *w.v.(1)* [WRECCHE *v.*], awake, arouse.

wuldor, *n.a-stem,* [WULDER]; glory 59, 155 *etc.*

wuldorblǣd, *m.a-stem,* [WULDOR + BLEAD]; glorious success 156.

wulf, *m.a-stem,* WOLF 206, 295.

wundenlocc, *adj.,* [WOUNDEN + LOCK]; with braided locks 77n., 103, 325.

wundor, *n.a-stem,* WONDER, splendour, 8.

wunian, *w.v.(2),* [WON]; dwell 67, 119.

wylle, see **wolde.**

wyrcan, worhte (*pret.sg.*) 65, **worhton** (*pret.pl.*) 302; *w.v.(1),* WORK, make, 8; *worhte,* was heading for 65n.

wyrm, *m.i-stem,* WORM; serpent, snake, 115.

wyrmsele, *m.i-stem,* serpent-hall, hell, 119.

Y

ȳcan, *w.v.(1),* [ECHE]; augment, add to, 183.

yldestan, see **eald.**

ymbe, *prep.w.acc.,* [UMBE]; around 47, 268.

yrre, *adj.,* [IRRE]; angry 225.